PUPIL'S BOOK

Arc-en-ciel 1

Ann Miller
Liz Roselman

MARY GLASGOW PUBLICATIONS

Arc-en-ciel Stage 1

Pupil's Book
Teacher's Book
Repromasters
Cassettes
Flashcards
Video
Video Guide
Assessment and Profiling pack
Chanterelles (songs)
Cover lesson pack
Fun with Arc-en-ciel 1 (computer software)

Illustrations
Hemesh Alles
Rowan Barnes-Murphy
Michel-Marie Bougard
Keith Brumpton
Phillip Burrows
Debbie Clark
Ian Foulis
Lydia Moscato

Design
Eric Drewery and Bob Vickers

Photographs
Adams Picture Library (page 150); Raymond Blythe (pages 119, 146); Bruce Coleman Ltd/Jane Burton (pages 37, 46); Bruce Coleman Ltd/Fritz Prenzel (page 46); Bruce Coleman Ltd/Hans Reinhard (pages 36, 37, 46); Colorific (page 66); French Picture Library/Barrie Smith (pages 66, 119); The John Hillelson Agency Ltd (pages 102, 146); The Hutchison Library (page 37); Mary Glasgow Publications Ltd (pages 11, 36, 66, 99, 119, 141, 146, 150); MGP/Frédéric Pitchal (pages 18, 31, 42, 69, 99, 150); MGP/Neil Waterson (pages 1, 10, 18, 88, 108, 111); NHPA/Stephen Dalton (pages 36, 37); NHPA/E A James (page 46); NHPA/Lacz Lemoine (page 46); NHPA/Gérard Lacz (page 46); Rex Features Ltd (page 7); Spectrum Colour Library (page 36); Frank Spooner Pictures (page 119); Tony Stone Worldwide (page 150); Tony Stone Worldwide/Jean-Marie Truchet (page 66); Syndication International (page 7); Topham Picture Library (page 119).

We are grateful to the following for allowing us to reproduce published material: *Salut!* (page 1); *Ouest-France* (page 7); *Télérama* (page 8); *Phosphore* (page 18); *Graffiti* (page 24); *Marie-France* (page 51); *Télé-Loisirs* (page 57); *Le Point, Marie-France, Top 50, Cool, Okapi, Première* (page 62); *Pariscope* (page 69); *Télérama* (page 74); Dictionnaires Le Robert (page 85); *OK! Magazine* (page 88); La Reash Couscous House, Greek Street, London W1 (page 150).

Every effort has been made to trace all the copyright holders but the publishers will be pleased to make the necessary arrangements at the first opportunity if there are any omissions.

The authors and the publishers would like to thank all those who have helped develop the Arc-en-ciel project, and particularly Marie-Thérèse Bougard.

© Mary Glasgow Publications
First published 1988. Reprinted 1989, 1990, 1992, 1993, 1994
ISBN 1–85234–174–2

© Mary Glasgow Publications
An imprint of Stanley Thornes (Publishers) Ltd
Ellenborough House, Wellington Street
CHELTENHAM GL50 1YD

Photoset in Linotron Palatino with Futura by Northern Phototypesetting Co, Ltd, Bolton and printed by William Clowes, Beccles

CONTENTS

Arc-en-ciel 1 covers Levels of Attainment 1 to 4 of the National Curriculum in all four Attainment Targets, and brings in all seven Areas of Experience.

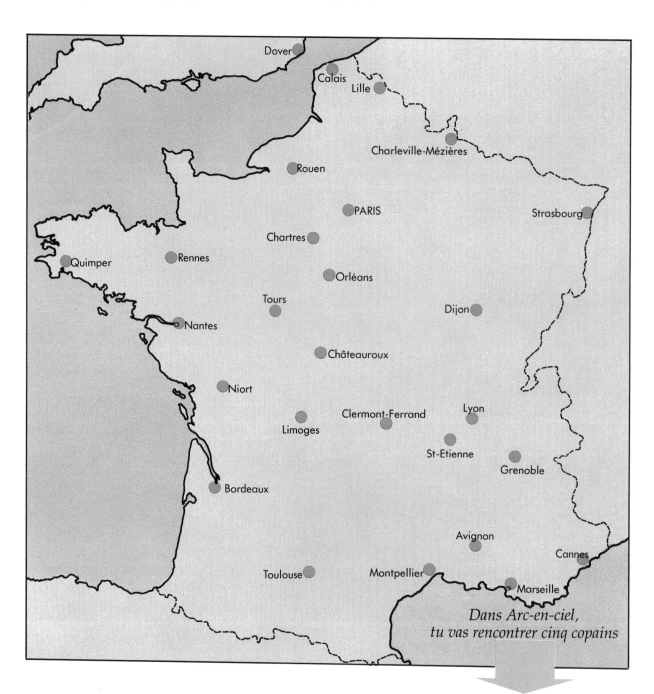

Dover
Calais
Lille
Charleville-Mézières
Rouen
PARIS
Strasbourg
Chartres
Rennes
Quimper
Orléans
Tours
Dijon
Nantes
Châteauroux
Niort
Clermont-Ferrand
Lyon
Limoges
St-Etienne
Grenoble
Bordeaux
Avignon
Cannes
Toulouse
Montpellier
Marseille

Dans Arc-en-ciel,
tu vas rencontrer cinq copains

Jean Lassègue   Sarah Jacobs   Sophie Thireau   Patrick Civardi   Katya Tedjini

Unité 1

 Bonjour!

 1. Now you will hear the same people again, but in a different order. Write down in your exercise book the numbers of the pictures in the order that you hear them.

2. Have you seen this yoghurt in your supermarket? Why do you think it is called *Bonjour*?

3. Look at the name of this French magazine. Do you think it is for young people or older people?

4. Listen to these people greeting you, and greet them back.

Sylvie   François   Hélène   Jérôme
Isabelle   Pierre-Yves   Amina
Céline   Fabien   Ludovic
Tchen   Djamel   Françoise

5. Work out which of these names are for girls and which for boys. Make a list of all the *prénoms* in your book, and against each one write *fille* if you think it's a girl's name, and *garçon* if you think it's a boy's name.

6. Now listen to a teacher reading out the names of children in her class. As you hear each name, write down the initials of that child in your book.

7. Look at all the surnames in this extract from a French telephone directory. Choose from among all the *prénoms* and *noms de famille* on this page and make up the names of six French characters (three girls and three boys).

ALEXANDRE Jean Pierre agricult...
AUGNET Georges agriculteur ....(35) 83.2
BEAUCAMP R agricult....
BOUQUET A cultiv....
BRÉARD Maxime march bestiaux ......(35) 85.42
CHAVANIEUX Henri cultivateur....
COQUATRIX M artis peintre....
FOLLIN Mme Camille infirmière

DELAUNE André entrepr électr (35) 27.0
DUCHAUSSOY transp et carrières(35) 27.0
FOYER DES PUPILLES (Aide Sociale à l'Enfance)...............(35) 27.0
GIRARDET E.........................(35) 27.0
HOORELBEKE P.......................(35) 27.0
ISAAC Janine infirm libre.......(35) 27.0

GOSSELIN Mlle Denise doct méd
4 r Dieutre.................(35) 71.06.
GOSSELIN D 2 r Forfait......→ (35) 73.30.
..................................(35) 70.60

MONVILLE ag..
PIGEON Mme Lucie...→ 2 à Anger

BERTIN J charron menuis...............44
BLONDEL Marcel 18
BLOSSEVILLE Julien 14
BOUDONNAT...........................34
BOYENVAL L..........................26
CAPRON Jean cultivateur.............11
CLÉON R camp........................22
CORNIER A tapiss....................33
COSTE Pierre Elie...................36
COSTE P agricul.....................20
DAVIN C.............................32
.Dé JEUNES—MARCELLAS G..............41
DESFOUGÈRES R Le Clos Normand.......21
DE TENEUILLE J Le Clos Pascal.......47
DUJARDIN F commerç...................1
DUJARDIN J-P boulang pâtiss..........9
DUJARDIN Jean cultiv................31
DUMUGUET L Le Village...............24
DUPUIS..............................40
HEIMANN J-P.........................45
IMPRIMERIE FLAHAUT H................27
JACQUES H...........................42
JOURDAN.............................19
KERCKHOVE A—M Les Courlis...........37
KRATZ DE VILLEMAIN Mme...............6
LEROUX A rte St Aubin...............46
LETHUILLIER Judith..................35
LEVASSEUR boucher....................3
LOSSET R............................23
MAIRIE ECOLE.......................12
PETIT C Bout de Haut................30

À la Maison des Jeunes

 8. Sarah's new friends have just arrived. Can you greet each of them by name? For example, *Salut, Sophie!* Listen to the tape first and say what you would say. Then write in your exercise book what you would put in the empty speech bubble.

Qui est-ce?

Bravo!

OBJECTIFS ATTEINTS

Now you can . . .

. . . greet someone	*Bonjour, monsieur/madame/ mademoiselle.* *Salut!*
. . . find out who someone is	*Qui est-ce?* *C'est . . .*
. . . find out someone's name	*Comment t'appelles-tu?*
. . . say what your name is	*Je m'appelle . . .* *Je suis . . .*

The sounds of French

Try and say this sentence with a French accent:

<u>Has your grandmother taken the horrible parrot home with her and sold her ship?</u>

Can you try and write down all the sounds that seem to be different in English and in French?

Here are some of the differences:

● There is no 'h' sound in French. Words which look the same as English words, like *horrible*, are pronounced as if 'o' was the first letter.

● The 'r' sound is produced with a different part of the mouth. It is produced at the back of the mouth by making the uvula vibrate. (If you open your mouth and look in a mirror you'll be able to see the uvula.) The English 'r' is pronounced in this way by people who come from Northumberland.

● French has nasal sounds: the French word for grandmother is *grand-mère*, and the part that is written *an* is said through the nose.

● There is no 'th' sound in French, so this is an English sound that French speakers may have difficulty with.

● When English speakers pronounce the 'o' sound in the middle of 'home' they begin with one sound and end up with

ch<u>â</u>te<u>au</u>   h – <u>o</u> – m – e

another. Try saying 'oh' and making it go on for a long time. What happens to your lips and your tongue? The French 'o' sound that you get in *château* doesn't change in the middle: you keep your tongue and lips in the same position all the way through.

● The 'i' in 'ship' would sound more like the sound in the middle of 'sheep' if it was spoken with a French accent.

The nearest sound to both of these in French is the sound in the second half of *habite*.

● There are some sounds in French that don't exist in English: the *u* sound in *tu* is made by putting your tongue in the position to say the *i* in *habite* and your lips in the position to say the *ou* in *vous*. You can achieve this by starting with the *i* sound and a big smile, and gradually bringing your lips forward and rounding them as if you were going to whistle.

9. You are going to hear some words which sound fairly similar in English and in French. You'll hear each word said three times. Decide which of the three words is the English word. Write down a), b) or c) depending on whether the first, second or third word is the English word.

Français	*Anglais*
Paris	Paris
table	table
télévision	television
cathédrale	cathedral
groupe	group
éléphant	elephant
photo	photo
film	film

TES OBJECTIFS	**In this unit, you will learn how to . . .**
	. . . ask people how they are
	. . . say how you are
	. . . greet someone in the evening
	. . . say goodbye/good night

 Ça va?

1. Look at the photographs in this newspaper. All of these people are asking each other how they are. Try and decide who would say *Comment allez-vous?* and who would say *Comment vas-tu?*

2. What is the order on the tape of these three programmes?

A Mesdames, messieurs, bonsoir.

B Mesdames, messieurs, bonsoir.

C Mesdames, messieurs, bonsoir.

3. What is the order on the tape of these four stills from films?

A "Au revoir"

B "Au revoir"

C "Au revoir"

D "Salut"

6.00

6.45	**TF1** BONJOUR LA FRANCE → 9.05	
	Emission de Jean-Claude Narcy.	
6.45	**A2** TELEMATIN → 8.30	

7.00

7.00	**C+** TOP 30 → 7.25	
	Présentation : Marc Toesca.	
7.10	**La5** LE MAGICIEN D'OZ → 7.35	
	Dessin animé. Reprise.	

4. There is a French television programme called *Bonjour la France*. Do you think it is broadcast in the morning or the evening? Why?

2 D
5. Write down the numbers of the dwarfs in the order that they speak.

 2 E
6. Madame Clément is looking after a party of French schoolchildren. Copy their names into your exercise book and note who is going into town this evening (Madame Clément says *Bonsoir* as they go past) and who is going straight to bed (she says *Bonne nuit* to them).

Édouard, Jérôme, Sophie, Jean-Paul, Nathalie, Virginie.

Bravo!

OBJECTIFS ATTEINTS

Now you can . . .

. . . ask people how they are
Ça va?
Comment vas-tu?
Comment allez-vous?

. . . say how you are
Très bien, merci.
Bof!
Et toi?
Et vous?

. . . greet someone in the evening
Bonsoir.

. . . say goodbye/good night
Au revoir.
Salut.
Bonne nuit.

Saying the right thing

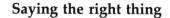

So there are two ways of saying 'you' in French. Why is that, Louis?

Well Victoria, it's because in French we like to show how well we know someone by the way we talk to them.

How do you do that?

We use 'tu' to our family and to people we know very well. We use 'tu' for children as well, even if we don't know them. And we use 'vous' for everyone else.

So the teacher says 'tu' to the child, and the child says 'vous' to the teacher.

That's right.

Comment allez-vous?

Comment vas-tu?

What happens when you're talking to more than one person?

We always say 'vous' then.

But what about English? Can't you show how well you know someone by the way you talk to them?

Yes my dear, as a matter of fact we can.

Comment allez-vous?

7. Here are two people. She is asking him if he has noticed anyone interfering with her car.

Make up speech bubbles for them which show, by the way that they talk, that they know each other well.

Now make up another set of speech bubbles which show that they are complete strangers.

Salut, grand-mère. Comment vas-tu?

Très bien, merci, chérie. Et toi?

TES OBJECTIFS

In this unit, you will learn how to . . .

. . . ask people where they live

. . . say where you live

. . . count to 100

---

 1. Listen to these people, who all live in the same street in Nantes, telling you their address.

Je m'appelle Agnès et j'habite un rue Lesage.

Je m'appelle Ludovic et j'habite deux rue Lesage.

Je m'appelle Jeanne et j'habite trois rue Lesage.

Je m'appelle Olivier et j'habite quatre rue Lesage.

Je m'appelle Sophie et j'habite cinq rue Lesage.

Je m'appelle Yann et j'habite six rue Lesage.

Je m'appelle Nathalie et j'habite sept rue Lesage.

Je m'appelle Ibrahim et j'habite huit rue Lesage.

Je m'appelle Isabelle et j'habite neuf rue Lesage.

Je m'appelle Delphine et j'habite dix rue Lesage.

---

 2. Now listen to the same people saying their address, but this time you've got to work out who's speaking: write the name of each person you hear in your exercise book.

3. Sarah is finding out where her new friends live. Listen to what they say, and find on the map the number that shows each person's street.

4. Look at this map of Nantes and see how many different words you can find that mean something like 'street' or 'road'. You can begin with *rue* but you'll find that there are lots more. Then look at the names of the streets. Many of them are named after famous people or places. *Voltaire* was a writer, and there is a street named after him.

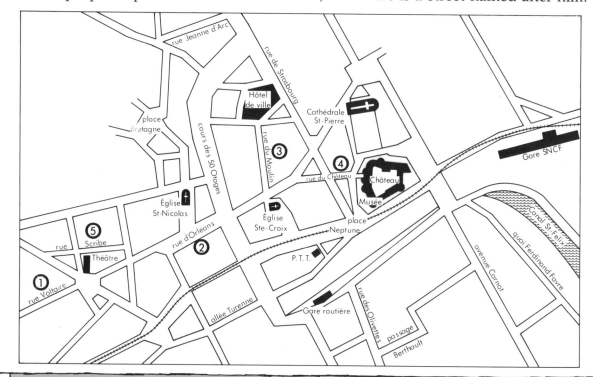

5. Listen to these people telling you where they live, and decide which bus they need to take to get to the *château*.

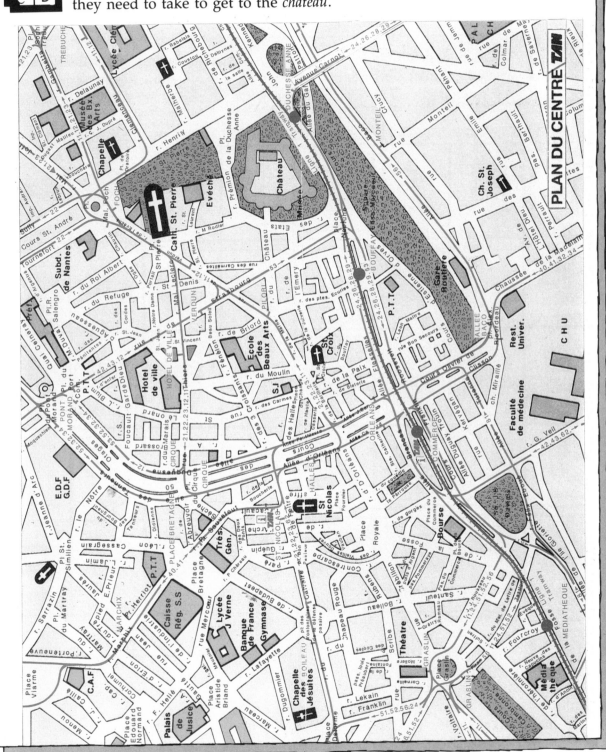

Unité 3

 6. Listen to the numbers of the rugby players being called out and note in your book which team they are in as they are called.

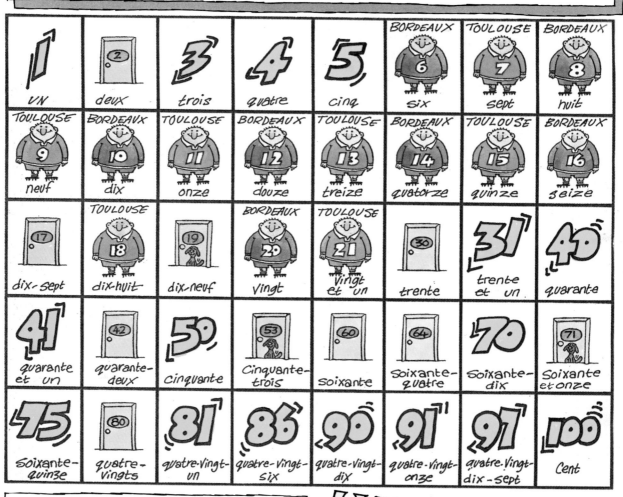 **7.** The new postman doesn't like dogs. He reminds himself of the houses where he thinks there might be a dog and calls out some house numbers. As you listen write *oui* (or O) if a dog does live there and *non* (or N) if there's no dog.

					BORDEAUX	TOULOUSE	BORDEAUX
1	2	3	4	5	6	7	8
UN	deux	trois	quatre	cinq	six	sept	huit

TOULOUSE	BORDEAUX	TOULOUSE	BORDEAUX	TOULOUSE	BORDEAUX	TOULOUSE	BORDEAUX
9	10	11	12	13	14	15	16
neuf	dix	onze	douze	treize	quatorze	quinze	seize

	TOULOUSE		BORDEAUX	TOULOUSE			
17	18	19	20	21	30	31	40
dix-sept	dix-huit	dix-neuf	vingt	vingt et un	trente	trente et un	quarante

41	42	50	53	60	64	70	71
quarante et un	quarante-deux	cinquante	cinquante-trois	soixante	soixante-quatre	soixante-dix	soixante et onze

75	80	81	86	90	91	97	100
soixante-quinze	quatre-vingts	quatre-vingt-un	quatre-vingt-six	quatre-vingt-dix	quatre-vingt-onze	quatre-vingt-dix-sept	Cent

 8. Béatrice has a list of telephone numbers to call. Which two numbers can you hear her call first?

40-80-17-40
40-31-75-50
42-18-13-81
35-21-86-15

9. Some French students are visiting your school. It's your job to finish off this list which says where they all come from. The envelopes that enclosed their letters to pen friends at your school give the information that will help you.

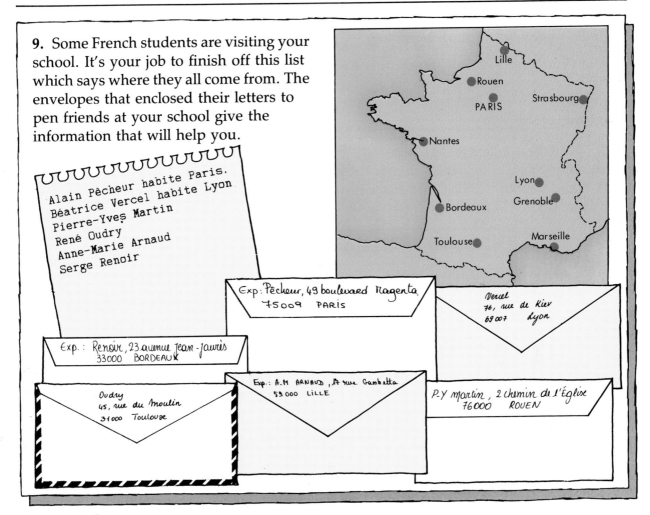

Alain Pêcheur habite Paris.
Béatrice Vercel habite Lyon
Pierre-Yves Martin
René Oudry
Anne-Marie Arnaud
Serge Renoir

Exp: Pêcheur, 49 boulevard Magenta,
75009   PARIS

Vercel
76, rue de Kiev
69007   Lyon

Exp.: Renoir, 23 avenue Jean-Jaurès
33000   BORDEAUX

Oudry
45, rue du Moulin
31000   Toulouse

Exp.: A-M ARNAUD, 17 rue Gambetta
59000   LILLE

P.Y Martin, 2 chemin de l'Église
76000   ROUEN

Bravo!

OBJECTIFS ATTEINTS

Now you can . . .

. . . ask people where they live — *Où habites-tu?*
Où habite . . .?

. . . say where you live — *J'habite . . .*
J'habite rue/boulevard/avenue . . .

. . . count to 100 — *un/deux/trois/quatre/cinq . . .*

Finding out where French is spoken

When you learn to speak French it means that you can speak to people from all over the world, not just in France – there are French-speaking areas in all five continents.

10. Read these letters that French-speaking young people from all over the world have written asking for pen friends in France. Look in an atlas to find where they come from. Then match them up with one of the young people from France. (Note: one French person doesn't manage to find a pen friend. Which one?)

Bonjour! Alger, le 30 Mars
Je m'appelle Djamel et

Je m'appelle Angélique.
J'habite à Tunis.

Je m'appelle Ousmane.
J'habite Dakar.

Je m'appelle Carole
et j'habite Fort-de-France

Montréal, le 27/1/88. Salut!
Je m'appelle Pierre.

Je m'appelle Elsa et j'habite Bern.

Je m'appelle Maimouna
J'habite à Bamako.

Salut! Je m'appelle
Nathalie et j'habite à Papeete.

Je m'appelle Amina.
J'habite Fort-Lamy.

Salut!
Je m'appelle Tchen.
J'habite Phnom-Penh.

Salut!
Je m'appelle Élise. J'habite Abidjan

Rabat, le 5 mai 1988. Bonjour.
Je m'appelle Hammou.

CORRESPONDANTS FRANÇAIS

Nom	Préférence
Jean Rivier	Canada
Luc Ferrari	Sénégal
Antoine Duhamel	Martinique
Danielle Schmidt	Tunisie
Olivier Jaubert	Algérie
Yasmine Massé	Suisse
Paul Guiraud	Côte d'Ivoire
Arnaud Messager	Mali
Sylvie Dupré	Maroc
Delphine Thomas	Kampuchéa
Yannick Satie	Belgique
Marie Martinet	Tchad
Agnès Arnaud	Tahiti

Unité 4

4 A *En classe*

1. Dépêchez-vous!

2. Bonjour, tout le monde. Asseyez-vous.

3. Sophie et Patrick, distribuez les cahiers.

4. La clarinette. Regardez l'écran.

5. Ouvrez vos cahiers et prenez vos stylos.

6. Dessinez la clarinette et écrivez 'la clarinette'.

7. Bon. Posez vos stylos. Écoutez la cassette.

8. Venez ici, tout le monde!

9. Taisez-vous!

10. Ne touchez pas à la clarinette!

11. Regardez et écoutez.....

4 B **1.** Now try and match up the commands that you hear on the tape to the above pictures. Write down the number of the picture that accompanies each command as you hear it.

Unité 4

C'est la rentrée!

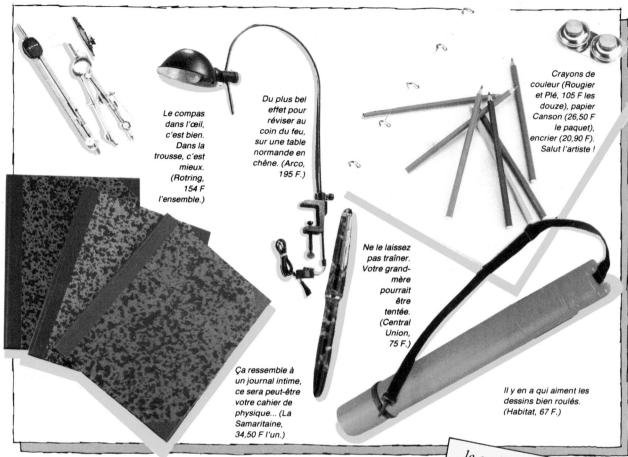

Le compas dans l'œil, c'est bien. Dans la trousse, c'est mieux. (Rotring, 154 F l'ensemble.)

Du plus bel effet pour réviser au coin du feu, sur une table normande en chêne. (Arco, 195 F.)

Crayons de couleur (Rougier et Plé, 105 F les douze), papier Canson (26,50 F le paquet), encrier (20,90 F). Salut l'artiste !

Ne le laissez pas traîner. Votre grand-mère pourrait être tentée. (Central Union, 75 F.)

Ça ressemble à un journal intime, ce sera peut-être votre cahier de physique... (La Samaritaine, 34,50 F l'un.)

Il y en a qui aiment les dessins bien roulés. (Habitat, 67 F.)

2. Look at these two photographs. Decide which one was taken in France. Copy the list into your exercise book and circle the names of the items which look unusual to you in the French photograph.

le sac/le cartable
le crayon
le stylo
la gomme
le cahier
la règle

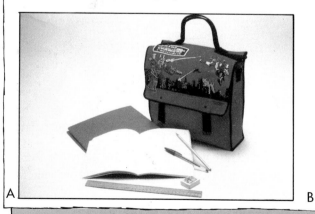

A

B

3. Try to decide who is saying what:

Taisez-vous!
Venez ici!
Regardez le cahier!

Ne touchez pas aux feutres!
Écoutez le monsieur!

4. There's a sale on in another shop and some of the items have been reduced in price. Copy out this list and when you hear the shop announcement advertising these reductions, make a note of the prices that have changed.

Le stylo:	13F
Le crayon:	3F
La règle:	6F
La gomme:	5F
La trousse:	16F
Les feutres:	19F
Le cahier:	14F
Le sac:	47F

5. Monsieur Langlais has bought presents for all his grandchildren. Can you decide which label should go on which present?

6. Julie has been having a hard time at school. Which of these sentences do you think she is saying to each of her 'pupils'?

Tais-toi!
Dépêche-toi!
Écoute!
Assieds-toi!

Bravo!

OBJECTIFS ATTEINTS

7. Now listen to Julie on the tape. In what order is she speaking to each of her pupils?

Now you can . . .

. . . understand classroom language

Dépêchez-vous/Dépêche-toi!   Distribuez les cahiers!
Regardez/Regarde!   Ouvrez vos cahiers!
Écoutez/Écoute!   Prenez vos stylos!
Taisez-vous/Tais-toi!   Posez vos stylos!
Venez ici/Viens ici!   Dessinez . . .!
Ne touchez pas/Ne touche pas!   Écrivez . . .!
Asseyez-vous/Assieds-toi!

le cahier/le stylo/l'écran/la clarinette/la cassette/le crayon/le feutre/

la trousse/le cartable/le sac/la règle/la gomme

POINT LANGUE

How can words be masculine or feminine?

● You have probably noticed that there are four different ways of saying 'the' in French.

l'école

la cassette

l'écran

les feutres

le cahier

● It's easy to know when to use *les* and *l'*.
– You use *les* when there's more than one thing (it's known as the **plural** form).
– You use *l'* in front of a vowel (a, e, i, o or u) and sometimes before 'h': *l'animal*, *l'éléphant*, *l'imbécile*, *l'orange*, *l'univers*, *l'histoire*.

● It's more difficult to know when to use *le* or *la*.

Words that you use with *le* are called **masculine** words. Sometimes they really are masculine, like *le garçon*, which means 'boy'. Words that you use with *la* are called **feminine** words. Sometimes they really are feminine, like *la fille*, which means 'girl'. But it's not usually so easy. For example, there doesn't seem to be anything particularly masculine about an exercise book (*le cahier*), and there doesn't seem to be anything very feminine about a cassette (*la cassette*).

We use the word **gender** when we're saying whether a word is masculine or feminine. For example, "What's the gender of *règle*?" "It's feminine."

● English is unusual because it doesn't divide words into masculine and feminine – most other languages do. Some languages have three genders, not only two like French. For example, German has masculine, feminine and neuter words.

Some research

Find some foreign language dictionaries in your school library or your local library. See how many languages you can find that have genders. Look up the words for classroom objects (pen, pencil, etc.) and look for a little '(m)' or '(f)' after the word. If you look in a German dictionary you'll find '(n)' as well, whenever there's a neuter word.

1. Write down
a) the names of the three gangsters
b) Rémy Salot's address
c) how much the taxi fare comes to.

2.

PARIS

FRANÇOIS

NANTES

ANNE-SOPHIE

JULIEN

This game can be played by two to six players. Choose one name in a square and decide which town you live in. Write down your name and town. Place a counter on the Paris square and take it in turns to throw the dice. Moving clockwise around the board move your counter as many squares as the number you have thrown on the dice. If you land on a person, the player on your left must ask you, Comment t'appelles-tu? and you must answer, Je m'appelle... giving the name of the person you have written down. If this is the same as the person you have landed on, you can cross off the name in your book. If you land on a town, the person on your left will ask you Où habites-tu? And you must answer J'habite... giving the name of the town that you have written down. If this is the same as the town that you have landed on, you can cross off the name of the town in your book. The winner is the first person to land on both their own name square and their own town square.

TOULOUSE

EMMANUEL

MARSEILLE

ISABELLE

BORDEAUX

CATHERINE

STRASBOURG

COPAINS COPINES

Try this reading activity!

3. These French students all want pen friends who live as close to them as possible. Can you pair them up? (There are different ways of doing this, so don't worry if your answer is not the same as other people's.)

Cher Salut!
Je m'appelle Hélène Arnaud.
J'habite Marseille.

Cher Salut,
Je m'appelle Jeanne MARTIN.
J'habite à Lyon.

Cher Salut,
Je m'appelle Michel Renoir.
J'habite Rouen. J'aime le

Cher Salut,
Je m'appelle Jean-Paul
Boulanger. J'habite
Toulouse.

Cher Salut,
Je m'appelle Véronique
Charef. J'habite Lille.

Cher Salut!
Je m'appelle Laure Jaubert et
j'habite Grenoble.

Cher Salut!
Je m'appelle Nicolas Weiss et
j'habite Strasbourg. J'aime
beaucoup la musique rock.

Cher Salut!
Je m'appelle Yasmine Pécheu.
J'habite Nantes. J'aime le sport.

Cher Salut!
Je m'appelle Luc Fitou.
J'habite Bordeaux.

Cher Salut!
Je m'appelle Nathalie
Queneau et j'habite Paris.

Try these listening activities!

4. You've got the names of the French exchange students, but your teacher has asked you to make a note of where they live. Match the names to the towns as you hear the students speak.

a)	Grégoire Klein	1 Marseille
b)	Béatrice Doinel	2 Nantes
c)	David Itard	3 Paris
d)	Pascale Zaïr	4 Bordeaux
e)	Olivier Lévêque	5 Toulouse
f)	Nabila Vercel	6 Lille
g)	Ludovic Talon	7 Grenoble
h)	Philippe Hugo	8 Lyon
i)	Ibrahim Naguib	9 Rouen
j)	Serge Oudry	10 Strasbourg

5. Here is a list of things that you may need for school. Copy it into your exercise book.

Now listen to this announcement in a French department store which tells you the prices of things you will need. Write down each price next to the item. (Be careful! You won't hear the items in the same order as they appear on your list.)

Stylo
Crayon
Feutres
Sac
Trousse
Gomme
Règle
Cahier

6. Listen carefully to these French teachers. Can you decide who they're talking to for each phrase that is said?

Unité 6

TES OBJECTIFS

In this unit, you will learn how to . . .

. . . say your age

. . . find out someone else's age

. . . say how old someone is

 Sarah and her younger brother and sister are starting at school today:

1. Here are Sammy, Lee and Sarah. Listen again to the conversations and say how old they are.

Je m'appelle Sammy. J'ai... ans.

Je m'appelle Lee. J'ai... ans.

Je m'appelle Sarah. J'ai... ans.

2. Look at the forms that Sammy, Lee and Sarah's teachers have to fill in. Copy the forms and fill in one for each of the children.

École Maternelle

Nom ....

Âge ....

École Primaire

Nom ....

Âge ....

Collège Victor-Hugo

Nom ....

Âge ....

3. Draw three columns in your book and write in these headings:
École Maternelle (Enfants de 2 à 5 ans) École Primaire (Enfants de 5 à 11 ans)
Collège Victor-Hugo (Élèves de 11 à 14 ans)

Sophie Bruneau
Romain Colin
Marie-Pierre Faure
Fabrice Faure
Malika Jaubert

Agnès Oudry
Laurent Platini
Nathalie Resnais
Juliette Tabard
Vincent Tabard

The children on this list have recently moved to the area. Listen to what they have to say on the tape and put their name on the list for one of the schools according to how old they are.

4. In this picture, find how many people say they are under 17 years old.

5. Look at these advertisements for three films on at the local cinema, then listen to six conversations which take place at the ticket office. For each conversation, write *oui* in your book if the person can see the film of their choice, or *non* if they cannot see the film because of their age.

EXPLICATION DES SIGNES

☐ Interdits aux moins de 18 ans
△ Interdits aux moins de 13 ans
◆ Recommandés aux très jeunes

donne. Avec Françoise Fa... Marie-Christine Rousseau, ... Ingrid Bourgoin. **Républic Cinémas 11ᵉ**.
J ◆ **FIEVEL ET LE NOUVEAU MONDE (An American Tail)**. — Amér., coul. (86). Dessin animé, de Don Bluth : A la fin du XIXᵉ siècle, une famille de souris russe émigre vers le Nouveau Monde. Lors de la traversée, le souriceau Fievel est projeté par dessus bord et aborde seul le continent américain. **St-Ambroise 11ᵉ, Saint-Lambert 15ᵉ**.

...onrad Veidt, Sydney Lorre. **3 Luxembourg 6ᵉ** (vo).
O △ **CASANOVA de Fellini**. — Italien, coul. (76). Comédie dramatique, de Federico Fellini : Les conquêtes et la solitude du séducteur dans l'univers baroque du grand cinéaste italien. Librement inspiré de « Histoire de ma vie » de Giacomo Casanova. Avec Donald Sutherland, Tina Aumont, Cicely Browne, Carmen Scarpitta, Mary Marquet, Daniel Emilfork Berenstein, Luigi Zerbinati, Hans van den Hoek. **St-Germain Studio 5ᵉ** (vo).

P ☐ **DE SANG FROID (The boys next door)**. — Amér., coul. (84). Policier, de Penelope Spheerys : Deux jeunes « paumés » de dix-huit ans attaquent un pompiste à Los Angeles. C'est le départ d'une suite d'agressions et de meurtres particulièrement violents. Avec Maxwell Caulfield, Charlie Sheen, Christopher Macdonald, Hank Garrett. **Forum Orient Express 1ᵉʳ** (vo), **UGC Montparnasse 6ᵉ**, **Ermitage 8ᵉ** (vo), **UGC Boulevard 9ᵉ**, **UGC Gobelins 13ᵉ, Images 18ᵉ**.
O **DOUBLE MESSIEURS**. — Franç., coul. (85). Comédie dramatique, de

6. Here is part of a letter that Sophie has written to her father in Africa:

Cher papa,

Nantes, le 3 septembre

Voici une photo. Patrick habite rue du Château. Il a 14 ans. Katya habite rue d'Orléans. Elle a 15 ans. Jean habite rue Scribe. Il a 14 ans. Sarah est anglaise. Elle habite rue du moulin. Elle a aussi 14 ans. Je suis

7. Here are four of Sophie's friends. Can you say how old each of them is?

Voici Patrick Civardi. Il a . . . ans.

Voici Katya Tedjini. Elle a . . . ans.

Voici Jean Lassègue. Il a . . . ans.

Voici Sarah Jacobs. Elle a . . . ans.

8. Draw a picture of your best friends or stick a photo of them into your exercise book. Write underneath who they are and how old they are.

TARIFS
Enfants (moins de 14 ans) ———— 5 FRANCS
Adultes ——————— 10 FRANCS

9. These ten pupils from the *Collège Victor-Hugo* are on a visit to the museum. Help the teachers to work out how much each pupil needs to pay and what the total bill will be. The two teachers must each pay the full adult rate.

Draw a grid in your exercise book and copy out the pupils' names and fill in their age when you hear it mentioned by the teachers.

Visite - MUSÉE DES BEAUX-ARTS
20 septembre

	Âge	tarif
1) Michèle Thomas		
2) Jean Lassègue		
3) Corinne Gallimard		
4) Katya Tedjini		
5) Patrick Civardi		
6) Sophie Thireau		
7) Stéphane Leclerc		
8) Pierre-Yves Mercier		
9) Philippe Vercel		
10) Sarah Jacobs		
Madame Hugo		
Monsieur Yersin		
Total		francs

Bravo! OBJECTIFS ATTEINTS

Now you can . . .

… say your age   *J'ai 13 ans.*

… find out someone else's age
                 Tu as quel âge?/Vous avez quel âge?
                 Il a quel âge?
                 Elle a quel âge?

… say how old someone else is
                 Il a 14 ans.
                 Elle a 15 ans.

POINT LANGUE

Using some English words to help learn some French words

10. Look at the menu for a French snack bar. Make a list of all the words that you recognise. Make a second list if you think that you can guess the meaning of the words.

11. Now listen to the tape and tick each item on your list when you think that you hear it said aloud.

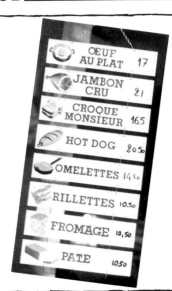

ŒUF AU PLAT	17
JAMBON CRU	21
CROQUE MONSIEUR	16.5
HOT DOG	8.50
OMELETTES	14.50
RILLETTES	10.50
FROMAGE	10,50
PATE	10.50

 Animal names

12. Write down in English the names of these ten animals. Now listen to the names of these animals being said in French. Put the number of the French word next to the English name as you hear it being said. See if you can say each animal's name like a French person.

Summary

● Many French and English words are the same but sound different when said aloud.

● If a French word sounds similar to an English word or is written like an English word, you can sometimes work out or guess its meaning in English.

● In other words you can often use English words to help you learn French words but you need to learn how to **pronounce** them like a French person.

● Listen carefully to how your teacher pronounces words and try to imitate them.

● See if you can say the names of some of the snacks and animals and pronounce them like a French person.

TES OBJECTIFS

In this unit, you will learn how to . . .
. . . ask what something is
. . . say what something is

 Au Musée d'Art Moderne

1. *Qu'est-ce que c'est?*
Find the French words that mean the following:

2. *Qu'est-ce que c'est?*
Copy out these four statements into your exercise book, then listen to the tape. You are going to hear someone introduce these four people. If you think that the boy is introduced first, put a number 1 by *C'est un garçon*, and so on.

3. Listen to the tape. You are going to hear recordings made at these five places. Write out the statements in the order in which you hear the appropriate noise.

4. Copy this map into your exercise book. Write a key for it which gives the names of the different places.

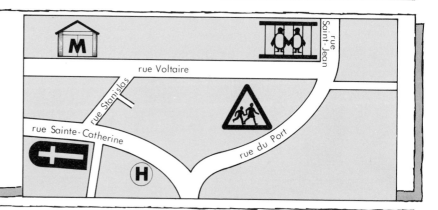

5. Listen to the tour that these tourists are making and mark on your map the route that they make around the streets.

6. This list tells you which animals you can see at the zoo. Work out which picture is which animal. When you have decided, write them in your exercise book in the order of the pictures. The first one has been done for you.
1 *C'est un tigre.*

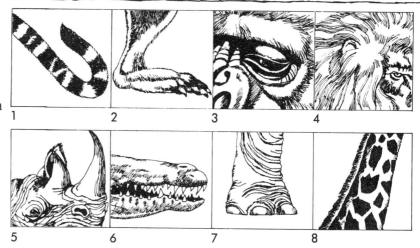

le crocodile	*la girafe*
le tigre	*l'éléphant*
le lion	*le rhinocéros*
le gorille	*le kangourou*

Bravo!

OBJECTIFS ATTEINTS

Now you can . . .

. . . ask what something is   *Qu'est-ce que c'est?*

. . . say what something is   For masculine words *C'est un . . .*
                                           For feminine words *C'est une . . .*

The French alphabet

 ● Like the English alphabet the French one has 26 letters. Listen to it.

a b c d e f g h i j k l m n o p q r s t u v w x y z

● Two of these letters *k* and *w* aren't used very much. When you do find them, they're usually in words that come from other languages. Have a look at the *k* and *w* sections in a French dictionary. You'll find words like:

k – koala   ketchup   kimono
w – walkman   week-end   western

 ● It's easy to learn the French names of the letters. You'll recognise some of them straight away. Listen to this first group:

f l m n s

 ● There's another group of eight which are almost as easy. Listen to them:

b c d g p t v w

● Did you notice those last two? What did you notice about the French name for what we call 'double u' in English?

 Listen to all those 13 letters again.

f l m n s b c d g p t v w

That's half the alphabet.

 7. Listen to these same letters again in a different order and write them down as you hear them.

● All languages use groups of letters as a convenient short way of naming things. In English we have such abbreviations as:
TV   l.b.w.   U.S.A.   P.E.   RAF   r.p.m.

● Here are a few French ones made up from the letters you've already met. You'll be able to see their meanings but how would a French person say them?

TV   B.M.W.   S.N.C.F.   Section B
Vitamine C   P.–S.

● So that's half the alphabet already. Now let's look at the other 13 letters.

 The vowels aren't very hard to learn. Listen:
a e i o u

● That just leaves eight others which need a bit more care:
h j k q r x y z
The name for *y* is '*i' grec* which means Greek 'i'.

 ● So if you put the whole alphabet together, it sounds like this.

● Groups of initial letters in French are similar to English ones but ordered differently since the order of the words is different.

8. Look at these four abbreviations and guess what the English versions are.
T.V.A.   ONU   U.R.S.S.   les rayons X

Unité 8

TES OBJECTIFS

In this unit, you will learn how to . . .
. . . say what pets you have
. . . say what you have in your packed lunch
. . . say what other people have
. . . ask someone what they have

 Here are some photos of children with their pets.

1 J'ai un chat. Il s'appelle Minou.
Anne-Laure, 12 ans

2 J'ai un chien. Il s'appelle Éric.
Olivier, 10 ans

3 J'ai un hamster.
Sophie, 8 ans

4 Nous avons un lapin. Il s'appelle
Chou-chou.
Suzanne, 13 ans, et Thomas, 11 ans

5 Nous avons des poissons rouges.
Thierry, 3 ans, et Pierre-Yves, 1 an

6 J'ai deux cobayes. Ils s'appellent Paul
et Mimi.
Pierre, 13 ans

1. Who has which pets? Copy the sentences below and complete them.

Anne-Laure a . . .   Suzanne et Thomas ont . . .
Olivier a . . .   Thierry et Pierre-Yves ont . . .
Sophie a . . .   Pierre a . . .

2. Listen to the tape of some pet animals. Write down in your exercise book what animal you think each one is. If you need help, have a look at the mystery photos below for some clues.

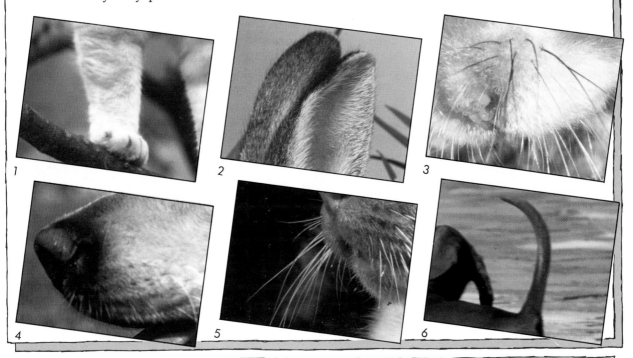

1

2

3

4

5

6

 3. Listen to the tape. You will hear all the children in the photographs on the previous page being asked about their pets. Write down in your exercise book the number of the photograph that you think goes with each recording. For example, if you think that the first recording is with the boys in photograph 5, write down: 1 . 5

4. Here is part of an advert for a pet fair in France. Name at least four animals which will be represented.

Le pique-nique

5. Here are all the foods mentioned in the story. What does everyone finally end up with?

L'anniversaire

6. It's Sophie's birthday. Four of her friends have bought some food and drink and are going round to her house to give her a surprise tea party. Listen to the things they have brought and look at the tea table later that day. What is missing from the table?

Bravo!

OBJECTIFS ATTEINTS

Now you can . . .

. . . say what pets you have	*J'ai un lapin.* *Nous avons un chat.*
. . . ask someone about their pet	*Tu as un chien?* *Vous avez un hamster?*
. . . say what you have to eat	*J'ai un sandwich.*
. . . say what other people have	*Les garçons ont des gâteaux.* *Ils ont un gâteau.* *Les filles ont des bonbons.* *Elles ont des bonbons.*
. . . ask someone what they have	*Qu'est-ce que tu as?* *Qu'est-ce que vous avez?*

Talking about more than one

● 'Boys and girls come out to play.' We know that this invitation is intended for more than one boy and girl because of the letter 's' on the end of the words girl and boy. We usually add an 's' to the end of a word in English to show that there is more than one of something. This is called the **plural**.

7. Make a list of English words which make a plural by adding an 's'.

8. Make a list of English words which make a plural in any different way.

● In French, like in English, many words are made plural by adding an 's'. Look back through unit 8 and find some of these.

● Some French words do something different.

un château	des châteaux
un gâteau	des gâteaux
un oiseau	des oiseaux

● In other languages there are quite different ways of talking about more than one.

In Italian, words that end in 'a' like *una bambina* (a little girl) end in 'e' in the plural, *due bambine* (two little girls). Words that end in 'o' like *un gatto* (a cat) end in 'i' in the plural, *due gatti* (two cats).

In Japanese, words don't change in the plural. But they always use a word like 'two', 'three', 'a few' or 'several' when they want to show that there is more than one thing.

9. Now you invent a different way of showing that there is more than one of something. You have been washed up on a small island with a group of people who all speak completely different languages.

You invent a new language that you can all understand and use. Make up your own words for the animals and things that you can eat on the island. Decide how you will let people know when there is more than one of something. (For example, one large fierce animal may not be a problem but a whole pack of them may require urgent attention.)

Write a brief phrase book for your new language and explain or give examples of your plural system.

Unité 9

Pas d'argent

1. Look at these advertisements. Complain to your teacher that you don't have these things or that you simply don't have any money: *Je n'ai pas d'argent.*

2. Look at the items that this snack bar is supposed to have. Listen to the conversation on the tape and say what the woman finally has for her lunch.

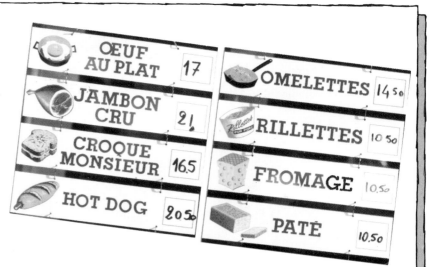

3. Katya has just had a small party. Whilst she and Sophie help her mother clear up, they find several items left around the house …

Write out these numbers in your exercise book and then write the name of the person who owns that item.

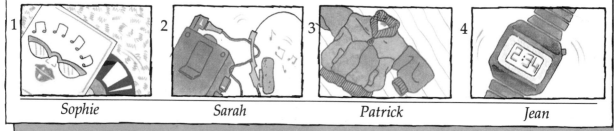

Sophie Sarah Patrick Jean

Cendrillon

Salut, Cendrillon. Ça va?
Regarde.... J'ai une invitation.

Salut, Cendrillon.
Ça va? Regarde.... J'ai une invitation.

Je n'ai pas d'invitation.

Au revoir, Cendrillon!
Dépêche-toi,..

Au revoir, Cendrillon

Salut, Cendrillon.
Ça va?

Non, je n'ai pas d'invitation

Viens ici.

Qu'est-ce que c'est?

C'est une invitation.

Mais je n'ai pas de robe.

Viens ici.

Mais je n'ai pas de moto.

Tu as un vélo?

Oui. C'est le vélo de ma demi-sœur.

Merci. Mais regarde! J'ai des pellicules.

Qu'est-ce que c'est?

C'est une bombe magique.

C'est le prince Stanislas.

Bonsoir. Je m'appelle Stanislas. Comment vous appelez-vous?

Je m'appelle Cendrillon.

Il a des boutons. J'ai une idée.

J'ai un yacht et une voiture.

Ppssssccchhtt!!

Qui a . . .				
une invitation?				
un vélo?				
un yacht?		*Copie cette grille*		
des pellicules?		*dans ton cahier.*		
des boutons?				
un problème?				

Qui n'a pas de . . .				
robe?				
moto?				

4. Copy out this grid into your exercise book and complete it.

Bravo!

OBJECTIFS ATTEINTS

Now you can . . .

. . . say what you haven't got	*Je n'ai pas de . . .*
. . . say who something belongs to	*C'est le disque/le walkman/ la veste /la montre de . . .*
. . . say you're sorry	*Je suis désolé(e).*

POINT LANGUE

Saying what you haven't got

● You may have heard the word **negative** used to describe the paper that photographers make prints from. If you look through a negative print, everything is the wrong way round. Light is dark and vice versa.

● When the word is used to talk about electricity, it refers to the minus side of a plug or battery that does not carry a live current.

● In each case it seems that a negative has something to do with opposites.

● When you hear the word used in a language study, it generally means that somebody doesn't want, doesn't do or doesn't have something. In unit 9 we saw that a lot of people didn't have various things.

● In English, there are many ways of making a negative statement. We will just look at one way here. Look at this example:

The girl could tell us:
'I've got an ice cream' or 'I have an ice cream'.
('I've' is really a short form of 'I have'.)

The boy could tell us:
'I haven't got an ice cream' or 'I haven't an ice cream'.
(The 'n't' is really a short form of 'not'.)

● In French, there is one main way of making a negative statement. It is to use the two little words *ne* and *pas*.

● Just as in English, the French also shorten some words, and the *ne* becomes *n'* if it is followed by a word beginning with a vowel (a, e, i, o or u) or an 'h'.

● Did you also notice that you don't need to use a word for 'a' or 'any'? The word *de* replaces *un, une* and *des*.

5. Now make up your own examples about some British people who have or don't have various things, then some French people who have or don't have various things. Don't forget to put in speech bubbles for what they are saying.

Unité 10

1. Here are all the objects that Ted hasn't got. Write down in your exercise book the numbers of the objects in the order that they are mentioned in the dialogue.
For example, object number 3 – the pen – will come first.

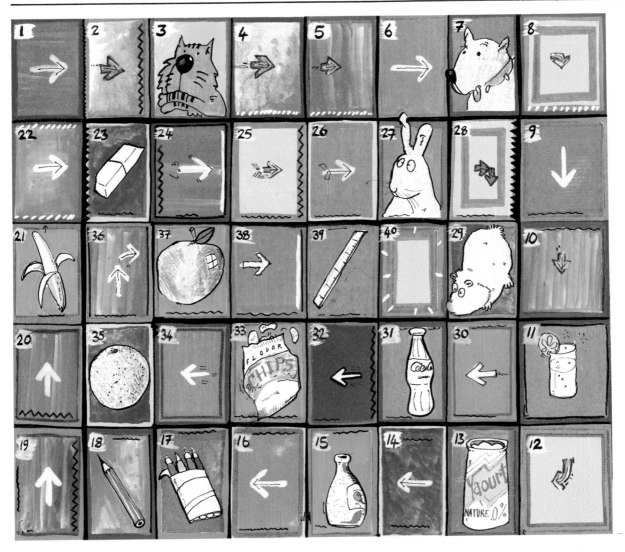

2. This game can be played by two to six people, but you also need an extra person who acts as a referee. Begin on the first square, and take it in turns to throw a dice. The winner is the person who gets to the fortieth square first. The things in the pictures belong either to (i) Marie, (ii) Pierre, (iii) Catherine or to (iv) Jean and Jeanne (these last two go everywhere together and share everything). If you land on a picture the referee will say: *Qu'est-ce que c'est?* You must answer *C'est un/une...* or *Ce sont des..* You must then try and guess who the item belongs to by saying *C'est le/la ... de ...* or *Ce sont les... de...* If you're right, the referee will say *Oui, il/elle a/ils ont un/une/des...,* and you can have another go. If you're wrong, the referee will say *Non, il/elle n'a pas de...* or *ils n'ont pas de...,* and you will have to go back to the square that you were on before you threw the dice. The referee should refer to page 48.

Try this reading activity!

3. A French school party on the Channel ferry have a problem with their packed lunches: half the contents are missing. You might be able to help, but first you need to know what they have and haven't got. Copy this list into your exercise book. Read the note that their teacher has written, then write *oui* against the things on the list that they've got, and put *non* against the things they haven't got.

Coca Cola
lemonade
sweets
biscuits
sandwiches
yoghurt
cakes
orange juice
apples
crisps

Ils n'ont pas de sandwiches et ils n'ont pas de chips. Ils ont des gâteaux, des bonbons et des biscuits. Ils n'ont pas de pommes. Ils n'ont pas de coca, mais ils ont de la limonade. Ils ont des yaourts. Ils n'ont pas de jus d'orange.

Try these listening activities!

4. Sophie is being given a quiz to see how many animal sounds she can recognise. You have pictures to show you the right answers. Each time she gets an answer right, write *oui* in your exercise book, and each time she gets one wrong, write *non*.

1

2

3

4

5

6

Answers to activity 2, page 47

Marie: le chat, la banane, le yaourt, le crayon.
Pierre: le lapin, la pomme, le jus d'orange, la règle.
Catherine: le chien, l'orange, le coca-cola, la gomme.
Jean et Jeanne: le cobaye, les chips, la limonade, les feutres.

Sandwich
gâteau
pomme
banane
orange
chips
bonbons
biscuits
limonade
yaourt

Sylvie
Luc
François
Hélène
Béatrice
Serge
Éric
Jérôme
Isabelle
Emmanuelle

5. Patrick was supposed to be packing lunch boxes for everybody, but he's left you to finish off. Copy out the list of items and the list of people into your exercise book, and listen as Sophie tells you what belongs to whom. Then draw a line from the item to the person's name.

6. *Le Père Noël* is doing a bit of checking up to find out what people already have, so that he knows what to give them for Christmas. He's just rung Jean to ask him what some of the children in his block of flats have and haven't got. He also needs to know their age. Copy the grid into your exercise book, and fill in Jean's answers on it.

Alain					
Catherine		*Copie cette grille dans ton cahier.*			
Jean-Paul					
Nathalie					

TES OBJECTIFS

In this unit, you will learn how to . . .

. . . say what school subjects you like and don't like

. . . ask someone what school subjects they like and don't like

. . . say what someone else likes and doesn't like

. . . thank someone for a present

 1. Listen to these advertisements:

 2. Now you will hear the advertisements in a different order. Can you match them up to these magazine adverts?

1

METTEZ-VOUS AU PARFUM.

THÉ À LA MÛRE SAUVAGE ÉLÉPHANT

2

JUMP :
LE KANGOUROU
C'EST
TOUT BOND !

JUMP : LA BARRE AUX CÉRÉALES ET AUX FRUITS.

3

 3. Listen to these extracts from horror films:

 4. Now you will hear them in a different order. Match them up to these pictures.

1

2

3

5. Tante Mathilde is really Sophie's great-aunt but her friends think of her as an aunt too. Today she is giving them all presents and they are thanking her. In some cases they really are pleased with their present but in others they are just being polite. You have to decide what their real feelings are by writing out the sentence that you agree with.

Sophie adore les poupées.
Sophie déteste les poupées.

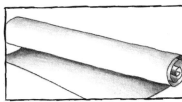

Jean adore les posters.
Jean déteste les posters.

Katya adore les rats.
Katya déteste les rats.

Patrick adore les ours.
Patrick déteste les ours.

Sarah adore les robots.
Sarah déteste les robots.

6. Here are two cuttings from a French magazine. Decide which one offers advice for consumers.

J'aime

En mars,

...D'énergie r
ver. Ces nou

A   **B**

Les consommateurs re-
cherchent la qualité ; c'est
aussi la préoccupation ma-

La nouvelle gam
plats cuisinés frais
Plaisir à la Carte, p
viandes et der

VOTRE HOROSCOPE

PAR HÉLÉNA RONDY

choix. Mais jouer la comédie, on le sait, n'est pas pour vous déplaire et en cet art vous êtes sublime !

Cancer (22 juin-22 juillet).
Hé oui, toujours mal luné ! Et des petits accrochages renforce-ront ce que l'on pourrait appeler un caractère de cochon. Il est dû aussi à la fatigue. Dans l'anfractuosité de votre chambre, profitez des week-ends pour vous reposer à fond et retrouver le sourire.

Lion (23 juillet-23 août).
Allez, courage, un Lion ne se laisse pas abattre quand les vents
t contraires. Il fait face en attendant qu'ils tournent
ce qui ne tardera pas. Promis.

7. Copy out this grid in your exercise book and fill it in to show how Sophie and Jean feel about their school subjects. Write their name into the squares that show their attitude to each subject.

	j'adore	j'aime	bof!	je n'aime pas	je déteste
les maths					
la musique		*Copie cette grille dans ton cahier.*			
l'anglais					
le français					
la géographie					

 8. Now use the same grid for Patrick and Katya. Listen to them talking about their feelings on the tape.

9. Do you know your partner well? Look at these groups of sentences about his or her likes or dislikes. Write down one from each group which applies to your partner. Then ask each other the questions (*Tu aimes les rats? Tu adores les rats? Tu détestes les rats?*) and score one point each time you guessed right. Use the same question to ask about maths (*les maths*), bats (*les chauves-souris*), crisps (*les chips*), and dolls (*les poupées*).

a)   (i)   *Il/Elle aime les rats.*
     (ii)   *Il/Elle adore les rats.*
     (iii)   *Il/Elle déteste les rats.*

b)   (i)   *Il/Elle adore les maths.*
     (ii)   *Il/Elle n'aime pas les maths.*
     (iii)   *Il/Elle déteste les maths.*

c)   (i)   *Il/Elle déteste les chauves-souris.*
     (ii)   *Il/Elle adore les chauves-souris.*
     (iii)   *Il/Elle n'aime pas les chauves-souris.*

d)   (i)   *Il/Elle aime les chips.*
     (ii)   *Il/Elle adore les chips.*
     (iii)   *Il/Elle n'aime pas les chips.*

e)   (i)   *Il/Elle n'aime pas les poupées.*
     (ii)   *Il/Elle aime les poupées.*
     (iii)   *Il/Elle déteste les poupées.*

Bravo!

OBJECTIFS ATTEINTS

Now you can . . .

. . . say what school subjects you like and don't like
     J'adore . . ./J'aime . . .
     Je n'aime pas . . ./Je déteste . . ./Bof!

. . . ask someone what school subjects they like and don't like
     Tu aimes . . .?

. . . say what someone else likes and doesn't like
     Il/Elle adore . . ./Il/Elle aime . . .
     Il/Elle n'aime pas . . ./Il/Elle déteste . . .

. . . thank someone for a present
     Merci, j'adore les . . .

Attitudes and intonation

● We can show how we feel about something without necessarily using words. This is what Sarah's brother, Lee, says when he sees something he really loves.

● Now look at Sarah, who doesn't like meat very much, responding to Lee's offer to get a hamburger for her.

● They both say the same thing, but they use a different tune, or **intonation**. Can you suggest the tunes that each of them might have used?

 ● Now listen to the tape and see if you were right.

---

10. Can you try and draw two wiggly lines to show the two different tunes?

 ● There are lots of other tunes.

● Listen to how Sarah answers Lee.

---

11. How does Sarah feel about these two pieces of information? How do you know? Can you draw the tunes that she uses?

Intonation in French

● French speakers don't use the same set of tunes as English speakers, although some are similar.

You've met one example of an important use of intonation, in English and in French – to show how sincere someone is.

---

 12. Try to describe, and draw, the difference in the way these two sentences are said.

---

 13. Listen to several people responding to a question, and see if you can work out what their attitude is and draw wiggly lines to indicate the tunes.

● One of the most important uses of intonation in speech is to make a difference between questions and statements.

---

 14. Listen to these sentences and decide which ones are asking you something and which ones are telling you something.

Unité 12

TES OBJECTIFS

In this unit, you will learn how to . . .
. . . give your opinion about something
. . . show that you agree with someone
. . . show that you disagree with someone
. . . talk about the likes and dislikes of groups of people

1. Write out the name of each person together with what they say about the picture, starting with the ones who like it best.

Bof !

C'est super!

C'est bien !

C'est moche!

C'est génial!

2. Patrick, Katya and Jean have each given the film a mark out of ten. Guess who gave the following scores:
a) Two   b) Five   c) Ten

C'est bien, ce film?

oh, c'est ennuyeux.

C'est pénible!

Non! C'est génial.

3. Now listen to this piece of music and listen to the group's opinions about it. Then re-order the symbols so that they're in the same order as the opinions you hear on the tape.

A   B

C   D

4. The group are talking about their school subjects. Try and rank them in order of popularity. Write out the names of the subjects in your exercise book, and give them a point every time someone says: *C'est génial!* or if someone says: *J'adore . . .*

C'est super!   *J'aime beaucoup . . .*

C'est bien!   *J'aime . . .*

Take off a point every time someone says:

C'est pénible!   or if someone says: *Je n'aime pas . . .*

C'est ennuyeux!   *Je déteste . . .*

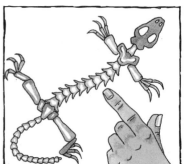

Bof! doesn't score any points but it doesn't lose any either.

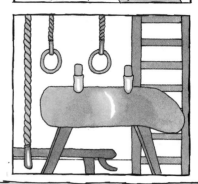

Vous aimez le sport?

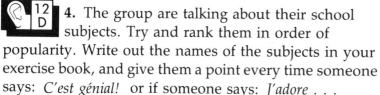

5. Patrick is interviewing his teacher to find out her views on sport. He makes his own views clear as well. Copy these symbols into your exercise book for the five sports he talks about, and draw two boxes beside each one. Write *oui* or *non* in each box to show whether firstly the teacher and then Patrick like the sport or not.

Le professeur   Patrick   Le professeur   Patrick   Le professeur   Patrick

L'histoire, c'est pénible

voir la page 58 ▶

PROGRAMMEZ VOS SOIREES TELE
SELECTION du 19 au 25 juillet

Vendredi

TF1 — JEUX
20.30 **INTERVILLES** — Saint-Chamond/Marmande. Présenté par Guy Lux, Léon Zitrone et Simone Garnier. Propose par Claude Savant.

VARIETES
22.15 **LE PRINTEMPS DE BOURGES** — Avec Indochine, Touré Kunda, Renaud, Fine Young Cannibals. Talk Talk. Véronique Sanson. Madness. Catherine Lara.

A2 — SERIE
20.35 **LE PRIVE (1)** — Un alibi de fer. D'Adolfo Aristarain. D'après l'œuvre de Vasquez Montalban. Avec Eusebio Poncela. Daniel Ceccaldi.

FR3 — SERIE
20.30 **HISTOIRES SINGULIERES (13)** — Le doux parfum de la mort. De Brian Clemens. Avec Dean Stockwell, Shirley Knight, Michael Gothard, Carmen De Sautoy.

CANAL + — FILM
21.00 ★★★ **LES AVENTURES D'ARSENE LUPIN** — de Jacques Becker. Avec Robert Lamoureux, Sandra Milo, Renaud Mary, Henri Roland, Daniel Ceccaldi.

Jeudi

TF1 — SERIE
20.30 **L'HOMME A POIGNE (1)** — de Herbert Asmodi. Avec Gustav Knuth, Eva Brumby, Dagmar Biener, Eos Schopohl, Rainer Hunold.

A2 — FILM
20.35 ★★★ **LES TROIS MOUSQUETAIRES** — d'André Hunebelle. Avec Georges Marchal, Bourvil, Gino Cervi, Jean Martinelli, Jacques François, Yvonne Sanson.

FR3 — TELEFILM
20.30 **BLEU-NOIR** — de Jacques Cornet. Avec Paul Barge, Daniel Rivière, Sophie Deschamps, Jenny Arasse, Philippe Rouleau.

CANAL + — FILM
20.35 ★★★ **CHARLIE BRAVO** — de Claude Bernard-Aubert. Avec Bruno Pradal, Jean-François Poron, Karine Verrier, Gérard Boucaron.

Mercredi

TF1 — SERIE
20.35 **LES AVENTURES DU JEUNE PATRICK PACARD (5)** — de Gero Erhardt. Avec Hendrik Martz, Wolfgang Kieling, Peter Bongartz.

A2 — TELEFILM
20.35 ★ **MARIE LOVE** — de Jean-Pierre Richard. Avec Béatrice Camurat, Roger Mirmont, Françoise Christophe, Catherine Rich.

FR3 — VARIETES
20.30 **FRANCOFOLIES** — Présenté par Jean-Louis Foulquier à La Rochelle. Avec Renaud, Indochine, Véronique Sanson, Touré Kunda, Alain Souchon.

Canal + — FILM
21.00 **JE SUIS PHOTOGENIQUE** — de Dino Risi. Avec Renato Pozzetto, Edwige Fenech, Aldo Maccione, Julien Guiomar, Michel Galabru.

Mardi

TF1 — THEATRE
20.35 **VIVE LA COMEDIE (4)** — Le major Cravachon. Pièce d'Eugène Labiche. Jesse et Lefranc. Mon Ismènie. Pièce d'Eugène Labiche.

FILM
21.55 ★ **LE VOYAGE** — de Michel Andrieu. Avec Victoria Abril, Christophe Malavoy, Victoria Cavallo, Michael Jacob, Assaf El Hakim.

A2 — FILM
20.35 ★★★ **LE TRAIN** — de Pierre Granier-Deferre. Avec Romy Schneider, Jean-Louis Trintignant, Nike Arrighi, Régine, Franco Mazzieri.

FR3 — FILM
20.30 **LES CHASSEURS DE SCALPS** — de Sydney Pollack. Avec Burt Lancaster, Shelley Winters, Telly Savalas, Ossie Davis.

CANAL + — SPORTS
20.00 **ATHLETISME** — Meeting de Paris. En direct du stade Jean-Bouin. Commenté par Robert Parienne et Charles Biétry.

Lundi

TF1 — FILM
20.30 ★ **DU SANG SUR LA PISTE** — de Ray Enright. Avec Randolph Scott, Robert Ryan, Anne Jeffreys, Peggy Moran, Broderick Crawford.

A2 — THEATRE
20.35 **LA BERLUE** — Pièce de Bricaire et Lasaygues. Mise en scène de René Clément. Avec Patrick Préjean, Claire Maurier, Pierre Vernier.

FR3 — FILM
20.35 ★ **L'EMPREINTE DES GEANTS** — de Robert Enrico. Avec Mario Adorf, Zoe Chauveau, Serge Reggiani, Andréa Ferréol, Patrick Chesnais.

CANAL + — FILM
20.35 **CA VA FAIRE MAL** — de Jean-François Davy. Avec Daniel Ceccaldi, Henri Guybet, Bernard Menez, Patrice Minet, Caroline Berg.

SPORTS
22.05 **TAUROMACHIE** — Corrida portugaise. Commentaires de Jean-Louis Burgat et Pierre Albaladejo.

Dimanche

TF1 — FILM
20.30 ★★★ **LA NUIT DES GENERAUX** — d'Anatole Litvak. Avec Peter O'Toole, Omar Sharif, Donald Pleasence, Tom Courtenay, Philippe Noiret.

A2 — TELEFILM
20.35 **LES ENQUETES DU COMMISSAIRE MAIGRET** — Maigret chez les Flamands. De Jean-Paul Sassy. Avec Jean Richard.

FR3 — SERIE
20.30 **TEMOINS** — Le Tour de France, son histoire, notre histoire. De Philippe Monnier et Bernard Lascazes. Textes d'Yves Berger.

CANAL + — FILM
20.30 **ON N'EST PAS DES ANGES... ELLES NON PLUS** — de Michel Lang. Avec Sabine Azema, Pierre Vernier, Georges Beller, Henri Courseaux, Marie-Anne Chazel.

Samedi

TF1 — SERIE
20.35 **LES OISEAUX SE CACHENT POUR MOURIR (3)** — de Daryl Duke. Avec Richard Chamberlain, Rachel Ward, Jean Simmons.

A2 — VARIETES
20.35 **TOUTES FOLLES DE LUI** — Présenté par Christophe Dechavanne. Avec Jeanne Mas, Sophie Duez, Talk Talk, Patrick Bruel, Françoise Hardy.

VARIETES
22.20 **LES ENFANTS DU ROCK** — Festival rock de Montreux. Avec Julian Lennon et les groupes Queen, Genesis, Depeche Mode, Pet Shop Boys.

FR3 — VARIETES
20.00 **SAC A DINGUES SURPRISE** — de Guy Montagné. A Saint-Malo. Avec Terry Shane, Jean-François Kopf, Gérard Surugne, Rita Mitsouko.

CANAL + — SPORTS
20.15 **FOOTBALL** — Coupe de la Ligue : Bordeaux/Racing de Paris. En direct d'Arcachon. Commenté par Charles Biétry et Pierre Sled.

Les parents: Monsieur et Madame Adjani
Ils adorent les films.
Ils aiment les téléfilms, les comédies, les jeux.
Ils n'aiment pas les émissions sportives, les variétés.
Ils détestent les séries américaines, les feuilletons.

Les enfants: Sélif et Nabila Adjani
Ils adorent les séries américaines, les émissions sportives, les jeux.
Ils aiment les films, les comédies, les émissions sur les animaux,
   les dessins animés.
Ils n'aiment pas les téléfilms.
Ils détestent les variétés.

6. Work with a partner, so that one of you has your pupil's book open at page 57 and the other at this page.

For the Adjani family, work out together the programme (or programmes)
a) the whole family will want to watch
b) no one in the family will want to watch.

7. Find two programmes that Monsieur and Madame de Bossis could watch, and two that they won't be watching.

Bravo!
OBJECTIFS ATTEINTS

Now you can . . .

. . . give your opinions about school subjects, sports and television programmes

> *C'est super./C'est génial.*
> *C'est bien.*
> *C'est ennuyeux./C'est pénible./C'est moche.*

. . . show that you agree/disagree with someone
> *Moi aussi./Moi non plus.*
> *Ah, moi je . . .*

. . . talk and ask about the likes and dislikes of groups of people
> *Nous aimons beaucoup . . ./Nous n'aimons pas . . .*
> *Vous aimez . . .?/Vous n'aimez pas . . .?*
> *Ils/Elles aiment . . ./Ils/Elles n'aiment pas . . .*

Slang
● So far you've learned four slang expressions in French: *C'est génial; C'est super; Bof!* and *Salut!*

● All of these are things that you'd say to someone you knew quite well, but you wouldn't say them if you were trying to sound posh.

8. How many ways can you think of to translate *C'est génial* and *C'est super* (they mean the same thing) into English? Make a list in your exercise book of English slang words that mean the same thing as *C'est génial* (for example, 'It's magic', 'It's wicked', 'It's well good', 'It's divine', 'It's magnificent') and divide them into groups:

a) Things that you would say.
b) Things that people used to say, but which have gone out of fashion (for example, in the sixties people used to say 'It's fab', but no one says this much now).
c) Things that very posh people would say.

9. If your parents or anyone in your family speaks another language, try and collect some slang words in that language that mean *C'est génial.*

10. This is a number of French slang expressions meaning *C'est génial* that have been fashionable over the past few years. If you have a French *assistant(e)* ask him/her to tell you which ones are still used and which ones are out of fashion now.

See if he/she can add any others to these expressions.

● Most languages have a lot of slang words that mean things like:

a) man, woman, work, money, food, drink, talk, etc.

But there are not many that mean things like:

b) chemistry, barometer, seagull.

11. Can you explain the reason for this? Try and think of as many slang words as possible for all the words in list a). Then think of some more English words that could go into list a) (words which are not slang themselves, but which have got lots of slang words meaning the same).

Unité 13

TES OBJECTIFS

In this unit, you will learn how to . . .

. . . ask and say what lessons you have on different days of the week

. . . say what day of the week it is

. . . talk about dates and birthdays

1. Draw up a schedule for a tour round France which would involve visiting a different town every day. You could begin:
lundi: Paris
mardi: Rouen
mercredi: . . .

2. You are in Senegal and want to know which are the days when you can get a flight back home to Britain. You ring up the airport, and get some information from the assistant. Write down the dates that you hear, and note down in English on what days of the week those dates occur. February 1st is a Monday.

	lundi	mardi	mercredi	jeudi	vendredi	samedi
matin	maths sciences	histoire français éducation physique	sciences français français	français maths	dessin anglais histoire	maths anglais travaux manuels
après-midi	anglais musique	travaux manuels géographie sciences		éducation physique éducation physique	maths français	

 3. Listen to Katya as she takes you through the class's timetable. Then listen to the sounds and write down whether it is morning or afternoon, and of which day.

 4. Look at all these items of school equipment. Make a list in your exercise book of the things that Katya needs to take to school on Mondays, Tuesdays and Wednesdays. Then listen to the cassette and make a list of the things that Djamel needs on Thursdays, Fridays and Saturdays. Make a separate list for each day.

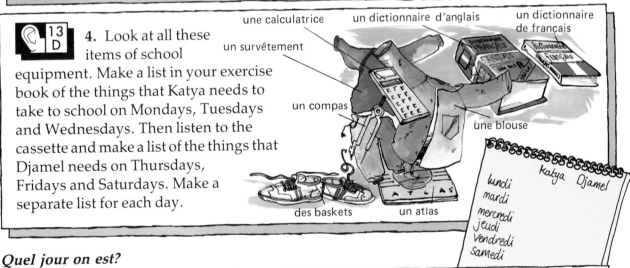

une calculatrice
un dictionnaire d'anglais
un dictionnaire de français
un survêtement
un compas
une blouse
des baskets
un atlas

katya Djamel
lundi
mardi
mercredi
jeudi
vendredi
samedi

Quel jour on est?

 5. Katya's and Djamel's mother is checking that they have all the equipment they need for school. Can you work out which day it is for each of them?

6. These magazines have got jumbled up and you are helping Katya to sort them out. As she says the name of each month, write down the name of the magazine that you have for that month in your exercise book.

7. Look carefully at these envelopes and read the letters to work out which letters should go into which envelope.

A

B

C

D

E

1
Le onze décembre.
Chère Sophie, comment vas-
tu ? Je suis à Paris

2
Le vingt-six janvier.
Cher Luc, ça va ?
Moi, je suis en

3
Le six janvier.
Cher Jérôme, j'ai un
chien ! Il s'appelle

4
Le quinze décembre.
Cher papa,
On a anglais et chimie lundi

5
Le seize décembre
Monsieur, j'ai
une voiture et je

BELIER
21 mars-20 avril

TAUREAU
21 avril-21 mai

GEMEAUX
22 mai-21 juin

CANCER
22 juin-22 juillet

LION
23 juillet-23 août

VIERGE
24 août-23 septembre

BALANCE
24 septembre-23 octobre

SCORPION
24 octobre-22 novembre

SAGITTAIRE
23 novembre-21 décembre

CAPRICORNE
22 décembre-20 janvier

VERSEAU
21 janvier-18 février

POISSONS
19 février-20 mars

8. Sarah has found out when everyone's birthday is. Listen and note down the dates. Then work out the birth sign for each of them.

9. Look at the calendar. Make a list of what makes it look different from a British calendar.

ouest france

JANVIER	FÉVRIER	MARS	AVRIL	MAI	JUIN
Jours augm. de 1 h 03	Jours augm. de 1 h 33	Jours augm. de 1 h 48	Jours augm. de 1 h 40	Jours augm. de 1 h 16	Jours augm. de 13 mn
1 V JOUR DE L'AN	1 L S¹ Ella 05	1 M S. Aubin	1 V S. Hugues	1 D F. TRAVAIL	1 M S. Justin
2 S S. Basile	2 M Présentation	2 M S. Charles le B.	2 S S⁴ Sandrine		2 J S⁴ Blandine
3 D Épiphanie	3 M S. Blaise	3 J S² Guénolé	3 D PÂQUES	2 L S. Boris 18	3 V S. Kévin
	4 J S⁴ Véronique	4 V S. Casimir		3 M SS. Phil./Jacq.	4 S S⁴ Clotilde
4 L S. Odilon 01	5 V S⁴ Agathe	5 S S. Olive	4 L S. Isidore 14	4 M S. Sylvain	5 D Fête-Dieu
5 M S. Edouard	6 S S. Gaston	6 D S⁴ Colette	5 M S² Irène	5 J S⁴ Judith	
6 M S. Mélaine	7 D S⁴ Eugénie		6 M S. Marcellin	6 V S² Prudence	6 L S. Norbert 23
7 J S. Raymond		7 L S⁴ Félicité 10	7 J S. J.-B. de la S.	7 S S⁴ Gisèle	7 M S. Médard
8 V S. Lucien	8 L S⁴ Jacqueline 06	8 M S. Jean de D.	8 V S⁴ Julie	8 D VIC. 45/F.J. d'Arc	8 J S⁴ Diane
9 S S⁴ Alix	9 M S⁴ Apolline	9 M S⁴ Françoise	9 S S. Gautier		9 V S. Landry
10 D S. Guillaume	10 M S. Arnaud	10 J S. Vivien	10 D S. Fulbert	9 L S. Pacôme 19	10 S S⁴ Landry
	11 J N.D. Lourdes	11 V S⁴ Rosine		10 M S⁴ Solange	11 S S. Barnabé
11 L S. Paulin 02	12 V S⁴ Félix	12 S S⁴ Justine	11 L S. Stanislas 15	11 M S⁴ Estelle	12 D S. Guy
12 M S⁴ Tatiana	13 S S⁴ Béatrice	13 D S. Rodrigue	12 M S. Jules	12 J ASCENSION	
13 M S⁴ Yvette	14 D S. Valentin		13 M S⁴ Ida	13 V S⁴ Rolande	13 L S. Antoine de P. 24
14 J S⁴ Nina		14 L S⁴ Mathilde 11	14 J S⁴ Maxime	14 S S. Matthias	14 M S. Elisée
15 V S. Remi	15 L S. Claude 07	15 M S⁴ Louise de M.	15 V S. Paterne	15 D S⁴ Denise	15 M S⁴ Germaine
16 S S. Marcel	16 M Mardi-Gras	16 M S⁴ Bénédicte	16 S S. Benoît-J.		16 J S. J.-F. Régis
17 D S⁴ Roseline	17 M Cendres	17 J S. Patrice	17 D S. Anicet	16 L S. Honoré 20	17 V S. Hervé
	18 J S⁴ Bernadette	18 V S. Cyrille		17 M S. Pascal	18 S S. Léonce
18 L S⁴ Prisca 03	19 V S. Gabin	19 S S. Joseph	18 L S. Parfait 16	18 M S. Eric	19 D S. Romuald
19 M S. Marius	20 S S⁴ Aimée	20 D S. Herbert	19 M S⁴ Emma	19 J S. Yves	
20 M S. Sébastien	21 D Carême		20 M S⁴ Odette	20 V S. Bernardin	20 L S. Silvère 25
21 J S⁴ Agnès		21 L S⁴ Clémence 12	21 J S. Anselme	21 S S. Constantin	21 M S. Rodolphe
22 V S. Vincent	22 L S⁴ Isabelle 08	22 M S⁴ Léa	22 V S. Alexandre	22 D PENTECÔTE	22 M S. Alban
23 S S. Barnard	23 M S. Lazare	23 M S. Victorien	23 S S. Georges		23 J S⁴ Audrey
24 D S. Fr. de Sales	24 M S⁴ Modeste	24 J S⁴ Cath. de Su.	24 D Jour du Souv.	23 L S. Didier 21	24 V S. Jean-Bapt.
	25 J S. Roméo	25 V Annonciation		24 M S. Donatien	25 S S. Prosper
25 L Conv. S. Paul 04	26 V S. Nestor	26 S S⁴ Larissa	25 L S. Marc 17	25 M S⁴ Sophie	26 D S. Anthelme
26 M S⁴ Paule	27 S S⁴ Honorine	27 D Rameaux	26 M S⁴ Alida	26 J S. Bérenger	
27 M S⁴ Angèle	28 D S. Romain		27 M S⁴ Zita	27 V S. Augustin	27 L S. Fernand 26
28 J S. Th. d'Aquin		28 L S. Gontran 13	28 J S⁴ Valérie	28 S S. Germain	28 M S⁴ Irénée
29 V S. Gildas	29 M S⁴ Gwladys	29 M S⁴ Gwladys	29 V S⁴ Catherine S.		29 M SS. Pierre, Paul
30 S S⁴ Martine	30 M S⁴ Amédée	30 M S⁴ Amédée	30 S S. Robert	30 L S. Ferdinand 22	30 J S. Martial
31 D S⁴ Marcelle	31 J S. Benjamin	31 J S. Benjamin	Printemps, 20 mars	31 M Visitation	Été, 21 juin

Le trois mars:
Mardi gras.

Le trois avril:
Pâques. J'adore
le chocolat !

Le premier mai:
la fête du travail.
Le muguet est fleuri.

Le vingt-cinq mai:
la sainte-Sophie.
C'est ma fête !

Le quinze juin:
c'est mon
anniversaire !

Le quatorze
juillet :
la fête nationale
Les feux d'artifice
sont super !

Le vingt-cinq
décembre :
Noël !

10. Sophie has kept a record of important dates for 1988. Work with a partner: one of you reads out one of the dates in words, and the other writes it down in figures.

Bravo!

OBJECTIFS ATTEINTS

Now you can . . .

. . . say and ask what lessons you have on different days
    On a . . . (lundi, mardi, etc.).
    Qu'est-ce qu'on a (mercredi, jeudi, etc.)?

. . . say what day of the week it is
    On est (vendredi, samedi, etc.).

. . . talk about dates and birthdays
    L'anniversaire de Katya, c'est le trois février.

Why is it so difficult to spell French verbs?

It's because most of the endings sound the same but they're spelt differently. Look...

Détester – to hate
je déteste – I hate
tu détestes – you hate (if you're talking to one person that you know quite well)
il déteste – he hates
elle déteste – she hates
on déteste – we hate
nous détestons – a more formal way of saying we hate
vous détestez – you hate (if you're talking to more than one person, or to an adult that you don't know very well)
ils détestent – they hate
elles détestent – they hate (if all the "they" are feminine)

How many of them sound the same as the 'déteste' in 'Je déteste'? Listen and I'll say them...

They all do except for the 'nous' and 'vous' parts.

Do you agree with Sarah? Listen again.

That means it's easy to say them, but you've still got to work at writing them.

I know – Monsieur Artaud gave me this exercise to do.

J'aime
Tu aimes
Il aime
Elle aime
On aime
Nous aimons
Vous aimez
Ils aiment
Elles aiment

But all verbs don't work like 'détester' and 'aimer' do they?

No. There are two other main groups, and then there are the irregular verbs with their own pattern, like 'avoir.'

AVOIR

J'ai
Tu **as**
Il/Elle/On **a**
Nous **avons**
Vous **avez**
Ils/Elles **ont**

Unité 14

TES OBJECTIFS

In this unit, you will learn how to . . .
. . . ask and say what the time is
. . . ask and say what time something happens

1. Look at these two pictures and write down in your exercise book what time you think it is. Then listen to the tape to see whether you were right.

2. *Quelle heure est-il?* Look at these photographs and decide which of them were taken at the following times of the day or night:

A   B

(i) Il est dix heures du soir.
(ii) Il est dix heures du matin.

C   D

(i) Il est trois heures et demie de l'après-midi.
(ii) Il est trois heures et demie du matin.

E   F

(i) Il est six heures du soir.
(ii) Il est six heures du matin.

3. Jean wants to set the timer on the video, but no one seems to have the right time. Write out the names of the people who tell him the time in the order that they speak. Then underline the name of the person who turns out to be right when Jean rings the speaking clock.

(i) Katya

(ii) Patrick

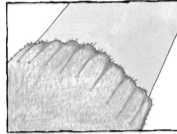

(iii) Sophie

(iv) Djamel

4. Draw the time that must be showing on the clock face for each of these pictures:

5. Now work with a partner. One of you has a copy of this book and tells the other one the time from each of these clocks. The other one doesn't look at the book, and has to draw a clock face that displays that time. When you've done them all, check that both sets of clocks say the same time. Then write the times down in words in your own exercise book.

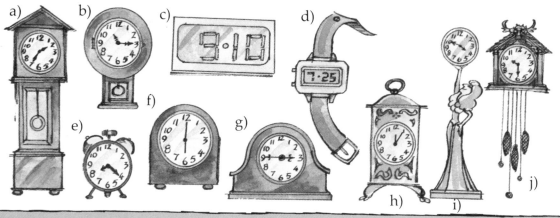

a) b) c) d) e) f) g) h) i) j)

6. Now work with a partner. Imagine you are in one of the places marked on the map. Assuming it is midday in London, work out what time it is and tell your partner, who then has to guess where you are.

For example: – *Il est sept heures.*   – *Tu es à New York.*

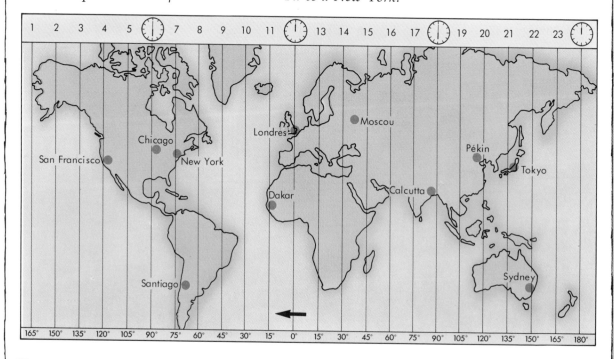

7. You'll often have to deal with the twenty-four-hour clock in France, so this will give you some practice. Monsieur Martin works for the French railways and is answering telephone enquiries from people who want to know train times. Work out where each of these people want to go, by comparing what he says to the sign in the station.

```
GRANDES   LIGNES        15 39
départ  voie  destination  et  principales gares d'arrêt
16h12  15  CHAUNY ST-QUENTIN CAUDRY CAMBRAI
16h27   6  MAUBEUGE LIEGE AACHEN WARSZAWA MOSKVA
16h46      MERU BEAUVAIS-GRANDVILLIERS ABANCOURT
17h13      AMIENS CALAIS DOUAI LILLE TOURCOING
17h45      LIEGE AACHEN KOLN HAMBURG KOBENHAVN
17h48      ARRAS DOUAI LILLE
17h30      CREIL CLERMONT-ST-JUST LONGUEAU AMIENS
17h36      CREPY ANIZY LAON NARLE VERVINS HIRSON
17h45      BRUXELLES BERCHEM DEN HAAG AMSTERDAM
17h47      COMPIEGNE NOYON CHAUNY ST-QUENTIN
17h53      PERSAN-BEAUMONT MERU BEAUVAIS
17h55      MAUBEUGE LIEGE VERVIERS AACHEN KOLN
17h58      ORRY CHANTILLY CREIL PONT COMPIEGNE
18h22      ORRY CHANTILLY CREIL ST-JUST
18h33      DUNKERQUE TOURCOING DOUAI VALENCIENNES
```

8. Here is an extract from a Parisian magazine which lists all the films on in Paris for one week. Choose a film and write down in your own exercise book the times of all the performances. Then read them out to your partner and see if he/she can work out which film it is.

> **Jean de Florette**
> Séances : 11h35 (Sf Dim et jours fériés), 14h05, 16h35, 19h05, 21h35. Film 30 mn après.
> **New York, New York** v.o.
> Séances : 11h30 (Sf Dim et jours fériés), 14h40, 17h50, 21h. Film 25 mn après.
> **37°2 le matin** Int — 13 ans.
> Séances : 11h25 (Sf Dim et jours fériés), 13h55, 16h25, 18h55, 21h25. Film 25 mn après.
> **Emmanuelle V** Int — 18 ans.
> Séance à 12h05 (Sf Dim et jours fériés), 14h05, 16h05, 18h05, 20h05, 22h05. Film 35 mn après.
>
> **70 MARIGNAN CONCORDE PATHE** 27-33 Av des Champs-Elysées. 43.59.92.82. M° Franklin-Roosevelt. Park angle Berri - Champs Elysées. Perm de 13h30 à 24h. Sam séance suppl à 24h. Pl : 35 F. Pour les — 18 ans et + 60 ans, du Dim 20h au Mar 19h. CV et étud du Mar au Ven jusqu'à 18h (sf fêtes). Pl : 25 F. Lun tarif unique : 25 F.
> **7 salles :**
>
> **Mannequin** v.o.
> Séances : 13h45, 15h25, 17h10, 19h, 20h45, 22h30. Film 15 mn après. Sam séance suppl. à 0h15.
> **Chronique d'une mort annoncée** v.o. Dolby stéréo.
> (Pl : 37 F et 26 F).
> Séances : 13h45, 15h50, 18h, 20h10, 22h20. Film 15 mn après. Sam séance suppl. à 0h30.
> **L'Eté en pente douce**
> Séances : 14h, 16h, 18h10, 20h15, 22h20. Film 20 mn après. Sam séance suppl. à 0h30.
> **Le Moustachu**
> Séances : 13h40, 15h40, 17h45, 19h50 ; 22h. Film 30 mn après. Sam séance suppl. à 0h05.

Bravo!

OBJECTIFS ATTEINTS

Now you can . . .

. . . ask and say what the time is   *Quelle heure est-il?*
Il est dix heures.

. . . ask and say what time something happens
À quelle heure . . .?
. . . à huit heures.

Asking questions

Questions in English

● How do you word a question in English if you want the answer to be:

a) either 'Yes' or 'No'?

b) a piece of information like 'At six o'clock', 'In Paris', 'Françoise' or 'A sandwich'?

Questions in French

● There are two ways of asking type a) questions in French:

(i) You can use an ordinary sentence but make your voice go up at the end. For example:

Tu habites Paris?
Vous êtes Monsieur Vedel?
Il est six heures?

9. Make up some questions for your partner by using ordinary sentences and making your voice go up at the end. After a few *Oui* and *Non* answers, your partner can see if it's possible to avoid using *Oui* and *Non* in his/her answers.

(ii) Or you can put *Est-ce que . . .* on the beginning of an ordinary sentence. For example:

Est-ce que tu habites Grenoble?
Est-ce que tu aimes les maths?
Est-ce que tu as douze ans?

The *Est-ce que . . .* at the beginning of the question is a way of letting the person you're speaking to know that there's a question coming up.

Can you think of ways that we do this in English?

● To ask a type b) question, where you are asking for a piece of information, you need a question word.

You've already met a number of question words in French.

10. See if you can match up these questions and answers:

Où habites-tu?
Qui est-ce?
À quelle heure est le film?
Quelle heure est-il?
Comment t'appelles-tu?
Comment vas-tu?
Qu'est-ce que c'est?
Quel âge as-tu?
Quel jour on est?

C'est un chien.
On est lundi.
Strasbourg.
J'ai quatorze ans.
C'est Bruno.
À huit heures et demie.
Très bien, merci.
Il est onze heures vingt.
Je m'appelle Anne-Laure.

Can you answer type b) questions with *Oui* or *Non*?

11. Can you make up symbols for all the questions in the list? When you have invented some, try them out on your partner. If you get sensible answers, you will know that your symbols work.

Unité 15

Salut, Francine! C'est super! Qu'est-ce que c'est?
C'est un saluki. C'est le chien de Chantal.

Edwina ne m'aime pas.

Ted ne m'aime pas.

1. Answer these questions:

a) *Est-ce que Ted aime les maths?*

b) *Est-ce qu'Edwina aime l'anglais?*

c) *Qui a une Cadillac?*

d) *Est-ce que Ted a une montre?*

e) *Est-ce que Ted aime Edwina?*

Calendrier perpétuel

2. Use this perpetual calendar to work out the day for any date between 1857 and 2036. For example, for 3 February 1990, find 1990 and follow it across to *février*. You will see the number 4. Add this to the number in the original date, 3 February: 4 + 3 = 7. Look up number 7 in column '**a b**' and follow it across to the day – *samedi*. *Le trois février, c'est un samedi.*

Now try these.

Le premier janvier 1988, c'est un . . .

Le premier mai 1996, c'est un . . .

Le quatorze juillet 2001, c'est un . . .

ANNÉES DE 1857 A 2036						JANVIER	FÉVRIER	MARS	AVRIL	MAI	JUIN	JUILLET	AOÛT	SEPTEMBRE	OCTOBRE	NOVEMBRE	DÉCEMBRE	a	b	JOURS
1857	1885	**	1925	1953	1981	2009	4	0	0	3	5	1	3	6	2	4	0	2	1	**	DIM
1858	1886	**	1926	1954	1982	2010	5	1	1	4	6	2	4	0	3	5	1	3	2	**	LUN
1859	1887	**	1927	1955	1983	2011	6	2	2	5	0	3	5	1	4	6	2	4	3	**	MAR
1860	1888	**	1928	1956	1984	2012	0	3	4	0	2	5	0	3	6	1	4	6	4	**	MER
1861	1889	1901	1929	1957	1985	2013	2	5	5	1	3	6	1	4	0	2	5	0	5	**	JEU
1862	1890	1902	1930	1958	1986	2014	3	6	6	2	4	0	2	5	1	3	6	1	6	**	VEN
1863	1891	1903	1931	1959	1987	2015	4	0	0	3	5	1	3	6	2	4	0	2	7	**	SAM
1864	1892	1904	1932	1960	1988	2016	5	1	2	5	0	3	5	1	4	6	2	4	8	29	DIM
1865	1893	1905	1933	1961	1989	2017	0	3	3	6	1	4	6	2	5	0	3	5	9	30	LUN
1866	1894	1906	1934	1962	1990	2018	1	4	4	0	2	5	0	3	6	1	4	6	10	31	MAR
1867	1895	1907	1935	1963	1991	2019	2	5	5	1	3	6	1	4	0	2	5	0	11	32	MER
1868	1896	1908	1936	1964	1992	2020	3	6	0	3	5	1	3	6	2	4	0	2	12	33	JEU
1869	1897	1909	1937	1965	1993	2021	5	1	1	4	6	2	4	0	3	5	1	3	13	34	VEN
1870	1898	1910	1938	1966	1994	2022	6	2	2	5	0	3	5	1	4	6	2	4	14	35	SAM
1871	1899	1911	1939	1967	1995	2023	0	3	3	6	1	4	6	2	5	0	3	5	15	36	DIM
1872	**	1912	1940	1968	1996	2024	1	4	5	1	3	6	1	4	0	2	5	0	16	37	LUN
1873	**	1913	1941	1969	1997	2025	3	6	6	2	4	0	2	5	1	3	6	1	17	**	MAR
1874	**	1914	1942	1970	1998	2026	4	0	0	3	5	1	3	6	2	4	0	2	18	**	MER
1875	**	1915	1943	1971	1999	2027	5	1	1	4	6	2	4	0	3	5	1	3	19	**	JEU
1876	**	1916	1944	1972	2000	2028	6	2	3	6	1	4	6	2	5	0	3	5	20	**	VEN
1877	1900	1917	1945	1973	2001	2029	1	4	4	0	2	5	0	3	6	1	4	6	21	**	SAM
1878	**	1918	1946	1974	2002	2030	2	5	5	1	3	6	1	4	0	2	5	0	22	**	DIM
1879	**	1919	1947	1975	2003	2031	3	6	6	2	4	0	2	5	1	3	6	1	23	**	LUN
1880	**	1920	1948	1976	2004	2032	4	0	1	4	6	2	4	0	3	5	1	3	24	**	MAR
1881	**	1921	1949	1977	2005	2033	6	2	2	5	0	3	5	1	4	6	2	4	25	**	MER
1882	**	1922	1950	1978	2006	2034	0	3	3	6	1	4	6	2	5	0	3	5	26	**	JEU
1883	**	1923	1951	1979	2007	2035	1	4	4	0	2	5	0	3	6	1	4	6	27	**	VEN
1884	**	1924	1952	1980	2008	2036	2	5	6	2	4	0	2	5	1	3	6	1	28	**	SAM

6.00	
7.00	
8.00	
9.00	maths
10.00	sciences
11.00	
12.00	DÉJEUNER

LUNDI MATIN

1.00	DÉJEUNER
2.00	anglais
3.00	musique
4.00	
5.00	
6.00	
7.00	

LUNDI APRÈS-MIDI

6.00	
7.00	
8.00	histoire
9.00	français
10.00	éducation physique
11.00	
12.00	DÉJEUNER

MARDI MATIN

6.00	
7.00	
8.00	maths
9.00	anglais
10.00	travaux manuels
11.00	
12.00	DÉJEUNER

SAMEDI MATIN

Write down one subject that you like (J'adore …) and one that you hate (Je déteste…) Throw the dice twice. This total gives you the time for Monday morning. The person on your left asks Quelle heure est-il? You answer. If this corresponds to a lesson the player on your left says On a… You reply C'est bien and move on to the next square. You can only move on if your time corresponds to a lesson. If you throw a lesson you said you liked, have an extra go. If it's one you hate, miss a go, but still move to the next square.

1.00	DÉJEUNER
2.00	travaux manuels
3.00	géographie
4.00	sciences
5.00	
6.00	
7.00	

MARDI APRÈS-MIDI

6.00	
7.00	
8.00	
9.00	sciences
10.00	français
11.00	français
12.00	DÉJEUNER

MERCREDI MATIN

1.00	DÉJEUNER
2.00	maths
3.00	
4.00	français
5.00	
6.00	
7.00	

VENDREDI APRÈS-MIDI

6.00	
7.00	
8.00	dessin
9.00	
10.00	anglais
11.00	histoire
12.00	DÉJEUNER

VENDREDI MATIN

1.00	DÉJEUNER
2.00	éducation physique
3.00	éducation physique
4.00	
5.00	
6.00	
7.00	

JEUDI APRÈS-MIDI

6.00	
7.00	
8.00	
9.00	français
10.00	
11.00	maths
12.00	DÉJEUNER

JEUDI MATIN

Try these listening activities!

15 B **3.** Copy the grid below into your own exercise book. Listen to the conversation and fill in on the grid as much information as you can about the times and days of lessons, and whether the two people speaking like or dislike them. (Use a five-point scale for the likes and dislikes: five points for liking a lot, four for liking, three for not really caring, two for not liking and one for hating.)

	LUNDI	MARDI	MERCREDI	JEUDI	VENDREDI	SAMEDI
8.00–9.00	Marie Pierre	Marie Pierre	Marie Pierre	Marie Pierre	Marie Pierre	Marie Pierre
9.00–10.00	Marie Pierre	Marie Pierre	Marie Pierre	Marie Pierre	Marie Pierre	Marie Pierre
10.00–11.00	Marie Pierre	Marie Pierre				Marie Pierre
11.00–12.00	Marie Pierre	Marie Pierre	*Copie cette grille dans ton cahier.*			Marie Pierre
12.00–1.30	Marie Pierre	Marie Pierre				Marie Pierre
1.30–2.30	Marie Pierre	Marie Pierre				Marie Pierre
2.30–3.30	Marie Pierre	Marie Pierre	Marie Pierre	Marie Pierre	Marie Pierre	Marie Pierre
3.30–4.30	Marie Pierre	Marie Pierre	Marie Pierre	Marie Pierre	Marie Pierre	Marie Pierre

15 C **4.** These are the television programmes for today. Listen to the conversation between Olivier and Béatrice and work out which programme they are going to watch together.

16.00

16.05 **La5** BUCK ROGERS ➡ 16.55
Série américaine. Rediffusion.

16.05 **M6** HIT HIT HIT HOURRA ➡ 17.05
Variétés-jeux.

16.55 **La5** LE MAGICIEN D'OZ ➡ 17.20
Dessin animé.

17.00

17.00 **FR3** FLASH INFOS ➡ 17.05

17.05 **FR3** FACE AUX LANCASTER ➡ 17.30
Feuilleton en vingt épisodes, en noir et blanc, d'après le roman d'Anne Mariel «Feux rouges à Beverly Hills». Précédente diffusion: juin 1971, 1ère chaîne.
Stéphanie : **Martine Brochard.** Chris : **Michel Le Royer.** Marie-Louise : **Darling Legitimus.** Alma : **Maria Machado.** Le commissaire Lenglen : **André Falcon.**
Troisième épisode. A Neuilly Stéphanie fait la connaissance de son beau-frère, un homme jeune encore, en qui on devine une grande expérience de la vie et qui cache, sous son assurance, une certaine timidité. Mais n'est-ce pas un comportement étudié ?

17.05 **M6** DAKTARI ➡ 18.00
Série américaine. Rediffusion.
Le mur de flammes (2). Jack, Paula et Judy sont prisonniers des deux chasseurs qui ont mis le feu à la brousse.

17.20 **C+** MAX HEADROOM ➡ 17.45

17.20 **La5** DANS LES ALPES

Try this listening/reading activity!

5. These are the programmes for last Saturday on one French channel:

13.00: Journal: **Informations**

13.35: L'homme qui tombe à pic: **Série américaine**

14.25: Bugs Bunny: **Dessins animés**

14.50: Les jeux du stade: **Émission sportive**

17.00: Cannon: **Série américaine**

17.50: Modes en France: **Magazine**

18.50: Des chiffres et des lettres: **Jeu**

19.15: Actualités: **Informations**

19.40: Affaire suivante: **Feuilleton**

20.30: Champs-Élysées: **Variétés**

21.55: Le voyageur: **Série américaine**

This week's programmes are similar, but there are a few changes. Listen to the conversation and note down anything in your exercise book that is different this week.

Try this reading activity!

6. Chantal has been picked for an important football team. A local television reporter has come round to interview her, but she is not in. Her brother, Marc, gives as much information as he can to the reporter about Chantal's timetable and her likes and dislikes. But he gets some of it wrong.

Write down the numbers of the sentences where Marc gives the wrong information.

Real timetable (including likes and dislikes)

1.30–2.30	maths ***	français *		maths***	français *	
2.30–3.30	anglais *****	géographie **		musique ****	biologie **	
3.30–4.30	travaux pratiques **	éducation physique *****		anglais *****	maths ***	

What Marc says

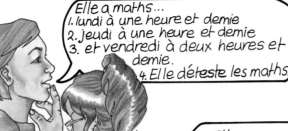

Elle a maths...
1. lundi à une heure et demie
2. jeudi à une heure et demie
3. et vendredi à deux heures et demie.
4. Elle déteste les maths.

Elle a anglais...
5. lundi à deux heures et demie
6. jeudi à une heure et demie
7. et vendredi à trois heures et demie.
8. Elle adore l'anglais.

9. Elle a musique jeudi à deux heures et demie.
10. Elle n'aime pas la musique.

Unité 16

TES OBJECTIFS

In this unit, you will learn how to . . .
. . . talk about your relatives
. . . ask someone about their relatives

1. Look at the Marquis's portraits again and see if you can remember who they are. Write out who each one is in your exercise book.

a)   b)   c)   d)   e)   f)

2. Patrick is telling Jean about the presents he has brought back from his holidays for some of his relatives.

Who is each gift intended for? Copy the sentences in the left-hand column into your exercise book and complete them using the words in the right-hand column.

1 *Le jeu est pour* . . .

son père.

2 *L'écharpe est pour* . . .

sa sœur.

3 *La chemise de nuit est pour* . . .

son cousin.

4 *Le train est pour* . . .

sa grand-mère.

5 *La boîte de mouchoirs est pour* . . .

son frère.

6 *Le canif est pour* . . .

son oncle.

7 *La cravate est pour* . . .

son grand-père.

8 *Le vase est pour* . . .

sa tante.

9 *La trousse est pour* . . .

sa mère.

10 *La lampe de poche est pour* . . .

sa cousine.

Les frères et sœurs

3. Listen to these people being asked about their brothers and sisters. Copy out the grid below into your own exercise book and fill in as much information as you can about each person.

Claire		Virginie
Pierre	*Copie cette grille dans ton cahier.*	Malika
Nathalie		Fabrice
Tchen		Vincent
Jean-Luc		Marie-Pierre

Les familles

4. Sophie and Sarah have very different families. On the tape you will hear them talking about their families. Look at their family trees. Sophie's has been filled in. Copy out Sarah's family tree in your exercise book and complete the information after hearing the tape.

L'arbre généalogique de Sophie

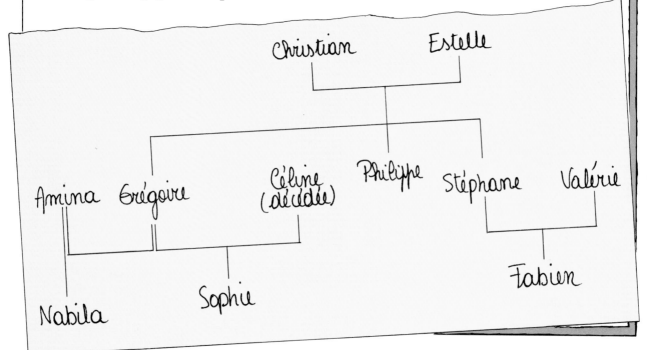

L'arbre généalogique de Sarah

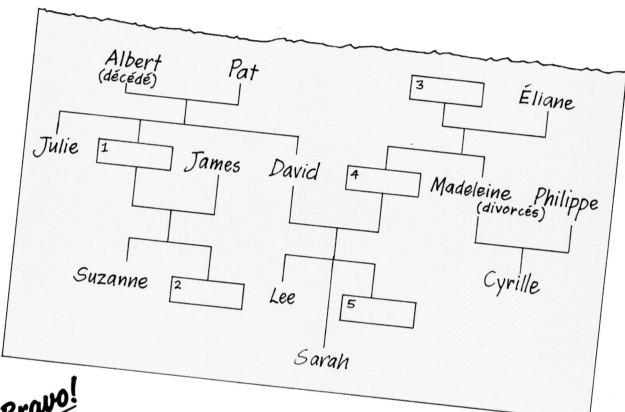

Bravo!

OBJECTIFS ATTEINTS

Now you can . . .

. . . talk about your relatives

> *Mon/ma . . . s'appelle . . ./a . . . ans.*
> *Mon/ma . . . est divorcé(e)/mort(e)/marié(e).*
> *Son/sa . . . est divorcé(e)/mort(e)/marié(e).*
> *C'est mon/ma . . .*

. . . ask about someone else's relatives

> *Tu as/vous avez un/une . . .?*
> *Ton/ta . . . s'appelle comment?*
> *Ton/ta . . . a quel âge?*

Saying something is yours (possessive adjectives)

● In unit 16 people talk about their relatives. You probably noticed that two words were used for 'my', that is, *mon* and *ma*.

● How do you know which word to use? It doesn't matter whether you are a girl or a boy. The important thing to remember is whether the person or thing that you are talking about is masculine or feminine. That is to say, whether it is a *le* or a *la* word. So you would say *ma sœur* for 'my sister' because it's *la sœur* and *mon frère* for 'my brother' because it's *le frère*.

● If we look again at the words for some of the relatives, see if you can sort them correctly into *mon* and *ma* categories:

oncle
tante
mère
père
grand-père
grand-mère

cousin
cousine
fils
fille

5. Try to invent your own system for having two words for 'my' in English. For example, you might decide that for everything that doesn't have an 'e' in it, you would say 'moy', but for everything that does, you would say 'may'. Then you would say things like this:

Visit to the beach

I took moy swimsuit. I parked moy car. Later, I realised I'd left may towel in the car. The wind was so strong that may newspaper was blown away and moy dog ran away with moy book. A big wave swept away may bucket and flooded may sandcastle.

● You may also have noticed in French that two words were used for 'your' and two for 'his' and 'her'. Look back at unit 16 and see if you can find them.

● In French, when you are talking about 'his' and 'her', it doesn't matter whether the person you're talking about is a boy or a girl. It is the person or thing that you're referring to that makes the difference.

6. Add some words for 'your', 'his' and 'her' to your system of talking about things you have.

TES OBJECTIFS	In this unit, you will learn how to . . .
	. . . say in which towns and countries your friends and relatives live
	. . . say what some of your favourite things are
	. . . say what someone else's favourite things are

1. Match these things with the person who gave them to Sophie.

les disques?

le petit déjeuner?

la carte postale?

Les copains et les copines
2. How many of Sophie's friends are mentioned in the story? Make a list of them in your own exercise book. For the boys, write: *Son copain . . .* and for the girls: *Sa copine . . .* For example:

Son copain Jean

Now make two lists of your own friends under these headings:
for your male friends: *Mes copains* and your female friends: *Mes copines*.

Mes choses préférées

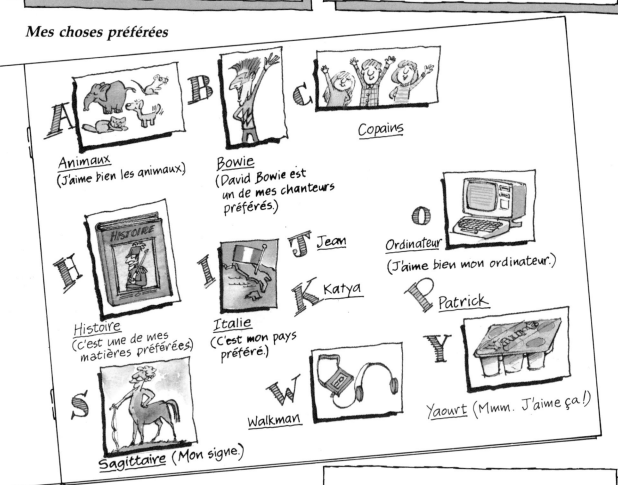

A — Animaux
(J'aime bien les animaux.)

B — Bowie
(David Bowie est un de mes chanteurs préférés.)

C — Copains

H — Histoire
(C'est une de mes matières préférées.)

I — Italie
(C'est mon pays préféré.)

J — Jean

K — Katya

O — Ordinateur
(J'aime bien mon ordinateur.)

P — Patrick

S — Sagittaire (Mon signe.)

W — Walkman

Y — Yaourt (Mmm. J'aime ça!)

3. Now write out in your exercise book an A–Z of your own favourite things.

4. Sophie, Jean, Patrick, Katya and Sarah all have friends and relatives in different countries. They have each received at least one letter or postcard from someone they know. Work out by looking at the letters and postcards who has received a letter or postcard and who it is from.

a)

b)

c)

d)

e)

f)

5. Match up the people saying where they live with their appropriate friend or relative:

a) *J'habite au Maroc.*
b) *Nous habitons en Angleterre.*
c) *J'habite en Italie.*
d) *Nous habitons au Canada.*
e) *J'habite en Espagne.*
f) *J'habite au Sénégal.*
g) *J'habite au Japon.*
h) *Nous habitons en Algérie.*
i) *J'habite en Côte d'Ivoire.*
j) *J'habite en Allemagne.*

1 *La copine de Sarah.*
2 *La grand-mère de Jean.*
3 *Les grands-parents de Katya.*
4 *Le copain de Patrick.*
5 *La copine de Jean.*
6 *Le père de Sophie.*
7 *L'oncle et la tante de Sarah.*
8 *Les cousins de Patrick.*
9 *Le copain de Sophie.*
10 *La copine de Katya.*

 6. Listen to the interview with the opera singer Céline Deneuve.

Complete the following summary about Céline Deneuve with words taken from the list below. Copy the correct sentences into your exercise book.

Elle est . . .
Elle habite à . . .
Elle a deux . . .
Elle aime . . .
Elle déteste . . .
Son film préféré est . . .
Sa passion secrète est sa collection de . . .
Sa ville préférée est . . .
Ses chanteurs préférés sont . . .

---

le cinéma/voitures/enfants/italienne/les acteurs/chanteuse/Paris/Cannes/Pavarotti et Placido Domingo/la musique pop/disques/ Blanche-Neige

Bravo!

OBJECTIFS ATTEINTS

Now you can . . .

. . . say in which town and country your friends and relatives live
  Mon copain/ma copine habite à Rome/en Italie.
  Mes copains/mes grands-parents habitent à Montréal/au Canada.

. . . say what some of your favourite things are
  Mon animal préféré/ma matière préférée est . . .
  Mes films préférés/mes voitures préférées sont . . .

. . . talk about someone else's favourite things
  Son chanteur préféré/sa ville préférée est . . .
  Ses animaux préférés/ses émissions de télé préférées sont . . .

Are dictionaries friends or enemies?

● There are three sorts of dictionaries where you can look up words you don't know.

English–French dictionary
You use this when you want to speak or write in French. You look up the English word for the French word you don't know.

French–English dictionary
You use this when you read or listen to something in French. You look up the French word you don't know and you find its translation, i.e. what it means.

French–French dictionary
This is the sort of dictionary French people use. In your English class, you probably use an English–English dictionary. It gives definitions, or rather, it explains the meaning of a word by using other words in the same language.

● When you have something to say or to write in French, it is tempting to look up the words you don't know in an English-French dictionary. But you must be careful: if you don't use it properly, a dictionary won't help you at all. You might find you make more mistakes. Look at this example:

---

7. You're talking to your partner about the food you like, but you have forgotten how to say 'chips' in French. What do you think the French word for it is?

● It is, of course, *frites*.
The first thing to do is to ask yourself: "How many different things can 'chips' mean in English?" It can be a bit from a piece of wood, a silicon chip as used in a computer, or a potato chip. If you know that the chips you are looking for are the ones that can be eaten, it is easier to find the right French word for them.

---

8. Try the same exercise with the following words and check with your teacher that you have found the right translation:

a) watch

b) record

c) game

d) cartoon

e) glasses

---

chip [tʃip] **1** *n* **(a)** *(gen)* fragment *m*; *[wood]* copeau *m*, éclat *m*; *[glass, stone]* éclat; *(Electronics)* microplaquette *f*. he's a ~ off the old block* c'est bien le fils de son père; to have a ~ on one's shoulder être aigri; to have a ~ on one's shoulder because ... n'avoir jamais digéré le fait que*...; *(Naut sl)* C~s charpentier *m*; *V* polystyrene.
  (b) *(Culin)* ~s *(Brit)* (pommes *fpl* de terre) frites *fpl*; *(US)* chips *mpl*.
  (c) *(Comput)* puce *f*, pastille *f*.
  (d) *(break) [stone, crockery, glass]* ébréchure *f*, *[furniture]* écornure *f*. this cup has a ~ cette tasse est ébréchée.
  (e) *(Poker etc)* jeton *m*, fiche *f*. *(fig)* to pass in *or* hand in *or* cash in one's ~s* passer l'arme à gauche*; he's had his ~s‡ il est cuit* *or* fichu*; when the ~s are down* dans les moments cruciaux; *(US)* in the ~s‡ plein aux as‡.
  (f) *(Golf)* coup coché.
  2 *cpd*: chip basket panier *m* à frites; chipboard *(US)* carton *m*; *(Brit)* panneau *m* de particules.
  3 *vt* **(a)** *(damage) cup, plate* ébrécher; *furniture* écorner; *varnish, paint* écailler; *stone* écorner, enlever un éclat de. to ~ wood faire des copeaux; the chicken ~ped the shell open le poussin a cassé sa coquille.
  (b) *(Brit) vegetables* couper en lamelles. ~ped potatoes (pommes *fpl* de terre) frites *fpl*.
  (c) *(cut deliberately)* tailler.

Extrait du Robert & Collins Dictionnaires Le Robert Édition 1987

TES OBJECTIFS

In this unit, you will learn how to . . .
. . . ask what someone is like
. . . say what someone is like

The *Oie d'Or* night club has been bought by Monsieur Alphonse. He is going to see his new employees. He is going to sack anyone that he thinks is unsuitable for their job.

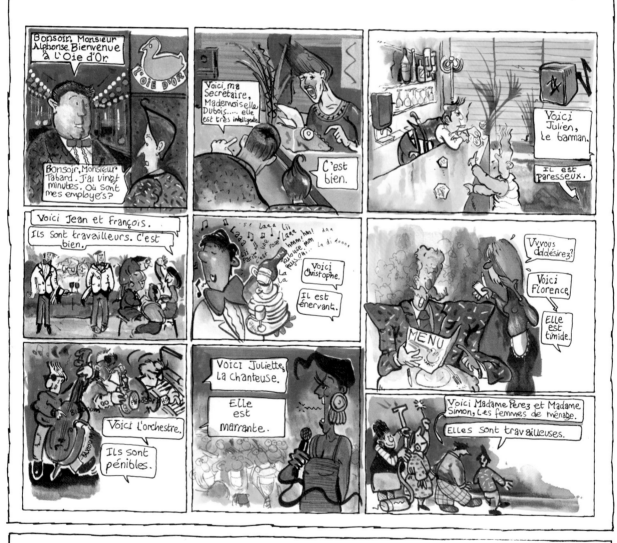

1. Make a list in your exercise book of all the words that Monsieur Alphonse and Monsieur Tabard use to describe people. Make another list of all the staff that you think Monsieur Alphonse has fired. Write out your reason beside each name.

Qui est-ce?

 18 A Sarah's mother is keen to know how she is getting on at school and with her new friends. As they look at some photographs she has taken of them, Madame Jacobs asks Sarah about her friends.

 18 B **2.** Listen again to the tape and say which person Sarah is describing.

3. Can you work out who these school reports belong to?

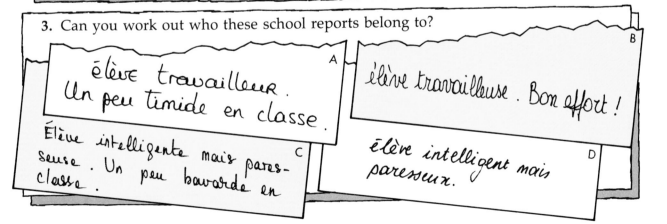

18 C Les bulletins scolaires

NOM GARAND	ANNÉE 19 19
Prénom Nadine	1er TRIMESTRE
Date de naissance 1 mai 1978	
Classe 6ème A	

DISCIPLINES	APPRÉCIATIONS DES PROFESSEURS
FRANÇAIS M	Élève intelligente, mais paresseuse
ANGLAIS M	Élève trop timide à l'oral.
HISTOIRE M	Bons résultats.
GÉOGRAPHIE M	Continuez!
MATHÉMATIQUES M	Encore des problèmes.
BIOLOGIE M	Bonne élève
DESSIN M	Travail très sérieux.
ED. MANUELLE M	C'est très bien!
MUSIQUE M	Élève sérieuse et intéressée

4. Listen carefully to the interview on the tape.

Say whether each of these sentences is true (*vrai*) or false (*faux*).

1. *Elle n'est pas forte en anglais.*
2. *Elle est forte en histoire.*
3. *Elle est forte en maths.*
4. *Elle est forte en dessin.*
5. *Elle n'est pas forte en musique.*

5. What are you like at school? Copy out a report form into your exercise book like the one shown above. First, write a report about yourself, then write a report about a friend in your class. Now swap reports with that friend and see whether you agree about each other!

Spécial astro

6. Look at this cutting from a French pop magazine. It mentions the three main qualities of Capricorns like David Bowie. The first two are 'stubborn' and 'brave'. What is the third quality?

7. Look at the pictures and listen to the story on the tape. See if you can work out in which order the pictures should go.

Bravo!

OBJECTIFS ATTEINTS

Now you can . . .

. . . say what people are like
*Il/Elle est intelligent(e)/sympa/paresseux(euse)/travailleur(euse)/
énervant(e)/bavard(e)/timide/marrant(e).*

. . . ask what people are like
Il/Elle est/Ils/Elles sont comment?

Pronouns

1. Michael Jackson met
2. Joan Collins at
3. The pub
4. She said to him: 'We were made for each other.'
5. He said to her: 'I love you my darling.'
6. And the consequence was: They lived happily ever after.

● Here are the first nine French pronouns that you will have found in this book.

Je – I
Tu – You (when you are talking to one person you know well)
Il – He or it (when the 'it' is a *le* word)
Elle – She or it (when the 'it' is a *la* word)
On – 'People' or often used to mean 'we'
Nous – We
Vous – You (when you're talking to more than one person, or one person whom you must address very politely or formally)
Ils – They (when the people or things are either all masculine or a mixture of masculine and feminine)
Elles – They (when the people or things are all feminine)

8. Look for these words in the game above and decide who they refer to: she, him, we, he, her, I, you, they.

● Words like 'I', 'you', 'he' and 'she' that replace names or nouns are called **pronouns**. We use them to avoid having to repeat the names.

9. Try to find the pronouns in the following advertisements.

A	B	C	D	E
Do you suffer from painful headaches? Take Hedeze. It really works!	Is she wearing Breezehold? It leaves your hair so natural.	I drink Slimsoup – It's got fewer calories!	We always drink Juicey juice!	They don't need a lift. They need the new Victor AZ. The car that wouldn't have let them down.

10. See if you can fill the blank spaces with the right French pronoun:

A . . . *avez mal à la tête? Prenez Hedeze. C'est efficace!*

B . . . *a Breezehold sur les cheveux? C'est si naturel!*

C . . . *bois Slimsoup. Il y a moins de calories.*

D . . . *buvons toujours Juicey juice.*

E . . . *ont besoin d'une nouvelle voiture.*

Unité 19

TES OBJECTIFS

In this unit, you will learn how to . . .

. . . say what someone's job is

. . . say where someone works

. . . say that someone doesn't work or is unemployed

 Katya's little sister is having a fancy dress party.

1. Which of the following jobs are mentioned in the story and in what order do they appear?

doctor factory worker teacher waiter secretary journalist actress
police officer barman housewife singer driver hairdresser

2. Look at these silhouette pictures. Write out in your exercise book what each person does for a job.

3. Jean, Sophie, Sarah, Patrick and Katya have accepted to be interviewed about where different members of their family work. Where does each person work, and what do they do? Write it out, starting *Madame Jacobs est caissière. Elle travaille dans un supermarché.*

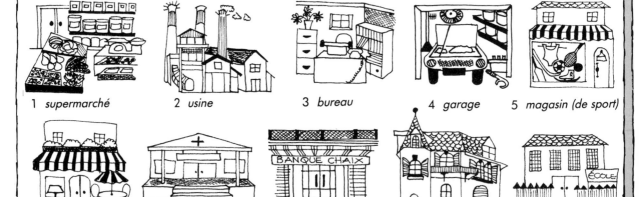

1 *supermarché*   2 *usine*   3 *bureau*   4 *garage*   5 *magasin (de sport)*

6 *restaurant*   7 *hôpital*   8 *banque*   9 *maison*   10 *école*

a) Madame Jacobs, la mère de Sarah
b) Monsieur Jacobs, le père de Sarah
c) Madame Lassègue, la mère de Jean
d) Monsieur Thireau, le père de Sophie
e) Monsieur Thireau, le grand-père de Sophie

f) Monsieur Tedjini, le père de Katya
g) Madame Tedjini, la mère de Katya
h) Abdel Tedjini, le frère de Katya
i) Monsieur Civardi, le père de Patrick
j) Madame Civardi, la mère de Patrick

chauffeur de taxi	*professeur*
propriétaire d'un restaurant	*docteur*
journaliste	*ménagère*
employé de banque	*ouvrier*
footballeur et propriétaire d'un magasin	*caissière*

Jean-Luc ne travaille pas. Il est au chômage

*Bonne chance! = good luck!

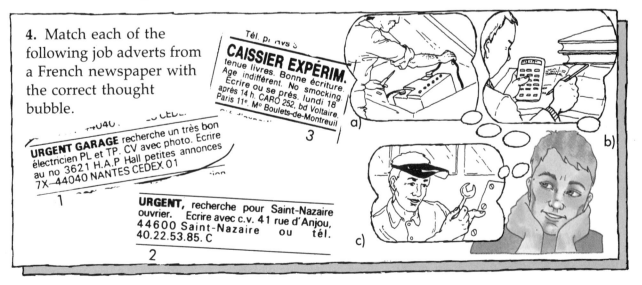

4. Match each of the following job adverts from a French newspaper with the correct thought bubble.

5. Play this game with a partner. Take it in turns to throw one or two dice to land in turn on each of the buildings. (It doesn't matter in what order you land on them.)

When you land on a place, tell your partner what your job is to score a point. For instance, if you land on the restaurant, you tell your partner: *Je suis serveur/serveuse.* If you land on the same place a second time, you can only score again if you can name a different job done in the same place. If you can't, you just stay there until your next go. If you land on the house you can also tell your partner that you are unemployed or that you don't go out to work.

The winner is the first person to have landed on all the places and named all the jobs.

OBJECTIFS ATTEINTS

Now you can . . .

. . . say what someone's job is

Il/elle est professeur.

. . . say where someone works

Il/elle travaille dans un bureau.

. . . say that someone doesn't work or is unemployed

Il/elle ne travaille pas.
Il est chômeur.
Elle est chômeuse.

POINT LANGUE

Using accents

– The first sort looks like this: ´. It is an acute accent. You find it over an *e* in words like *école* and *éléphant*. It tells you the *e* is pronounced in a special way. You need to have a sort of smile on your face, then say it like the letter 'a'.

– Another accent looks like this: ` . This one is called a grave accent. It is often over an *e* as well, but this time you pronounce it like the word 'air' in English.
– Like the one I saw on *mère*.

6. See if you can make a list of names that have these accents in them, and practise saying them.

– But you sometimes find these over other letters too. Then it shows that two words may sound the same, but have a different meaning. Take the words *a* and *à*: the first means 'has', like *elle a un chien*, and the second one means 'in' or 'at', like *j'habite à Nantes*. They sound the same, but they don't mean the same.
– What about the little hat?

– It is called a circumflex and it often shows that the Latin word the word comes from had an *s* in it. For instance, *fête* comes from the word *festum* in Latin, which means a holiday or a feast. It is the same for the English word 'festival'.

7. Here are some French words with a circumflex in them. Try putting an *s* in place of the accent, then finding an English word with a similar meaning.

hôte, hôpital, pâtisserie, enquête, château

– What about the squiggle, or upside down g?
– It is called a cedilla. It tells you that instead of pronouncing a 'c' like a 'k', you pronounce it like an 's'. We speak 'fransais', not 'frankais'.

8. If you look in a dictionary for the words Christmas, corn and selfish, you will find the one accent Lee didn't ask about.

9. The signwriter hasn't finished his job. Copy out the words below and fill in any accents that you think he missed off.
musee, theatre, cinema, hopital, college

Unité
20

1. Look at the last picture. Say who all the people are, and give as much information about them as you can. For example, write in your exercise book: 1. *Nathalie: c'est la sœur de Patrick. Elle est secrétaire.*

Try this reading activity!

2. The three members of the group *Ange Noir* have been asked about their favourite things. Write down the names of the three members of the group, and then list the number associated with the thing that each one likes best.

Michèle Lambert: Quelle est ta voiture préférée?

Romain: Moi, j'aime bien ma Renault 5. Mais je préfère les Mercédes.

Salif: Moi, j'ai une Peugeot 505. Elle est très belle.

Laurent: Moi, je n'aime pas les voitures. Je préfère les motos.

M.L.: Quel est ton animal préféré?

R: Les rats. J'adore les rats.

S: Moi, j'aime beaucoup les chats. J'ai deux chats à la maison.

L: Les animaux? Bof! Je ne sais pas.

M.L.: Quel est ton passe-temps préféré?

R: Le football.

S: Euh . . . le cinéma.

L: Mon passe-temps préféré, c'est les filles.

M.L.: Quelle est ton émission de télévision préférée?

R: Euh . . . je ne sais pas. J'aime beaucoup les émissions de sport, mais je préfère les dessins animés. Oui – les dessins animés.

S: Mon émission préférée, c'est les actualités. Et je déteste les jeux.

L: Moi aussi, je déteste les jeux. J'aime bien les dessins animés mais mon émission préférée, c'est les variétés.

Try these reading and listening activities!

 3. Two young people have applied to a computer dating agency for a boyfriend and girlfriend. You are going to hear them talking about the boy or girl of their dreams.

Here are the dossiers of six young people who have also applied to the same agency. Read them carefully before listening to the tape. As you listen to the tape, make notes and pick out the boy and the girl from the dossiers who would seem to fit the description of the dream boy and dream girl most closely.

Dossiers

Filles

1 Florence DUVAL
Je suis grande. Je suis assez marrante, mais je suis paresseuse. Je travaille dans un bureau. Je suis secrétaire. J'aime la musique, les chats et les chiens. J'aime aussi les enfants.

2 Estelle MORAND
Je suis petite, mais forte. Je suis bavarde. Je suis professeur. Je travaille dans une école. J'aime les enfants, le sport et la musique.

3 KARINE LAGRANGE
Je suis petite et je suis assez timide. Je travaille dans un hôpital. J'aime la télévision, la musique, mon jardin et mes lapins.

Garçons

1 Nicolas MARTIN
Je suis grand. Je suis assez timide. Je travaille dans un supermarché. J'aime le sport, la télévision, et les grands chiens.

2 Ludovic CENSTER
Je suis petit, mais fort. Je suis bavard. Je travaille dans une usine. Je suis ouvrier. J'aime mes copains, ma voiture et mon jardin.

3 Frédéric MARCHAND
Je suis grand. Je travaille dans un grand garage. J'aime les voitures, la musique, le football et le rugby.

Try these reading and listening activities!

4. Ariane Florent, the famous film star, likes to keep her private life a secret, and has a tendency to keep changing the information she gives. Read this article about her and then listen to the tape. Then write out only those facts which are the same in the article and on the tape.

> ### Ariane Florent, une nouvelle star
>
> *Elle s'appelle Ariane, elle a dix-neuf ans et elle habite Paris. Sa mère est actrice: elle s'appelle Nadja. Ses parents sont divorcés. Elle n'est pas mariée mais elle a un copain: c'est le chanteur Marco. Son passe-temps préféré, c'est la musique. Elle est très belle, un peu timide, un peu sauvage.*

5. Your teacher has some application forms from some students who would like a pen friend and you are helping her to sort them out. You have a list of names and need information about where each student lives and their age. Copy this grid into your exercise book and as you hear your teacher speak, write the name of the student under the name of the country where they live together with their age.

Suzy Konankro
Aziz Kahli
Amadou Seck
Nabila Charif
Étienne Brunel
Luisa Ramos

Copie cette grille dans ton cahier.

Côte d'Ivoire	Canada	Algérie	Maroc	Sénégal	Espagne

Try this writing activity!

6. Write a magazine article about your favourite person. Say where he/she comes from, what he/she is like, what he/she does for a living and list some of his/her favourite things.

TES OBJECTIFS

In this unit, you will learn how to . . .

. . . say what clothes there are in your wardrobe

. . . say what is not there

. . . say where things are

. . . say what colour something is

Le défilé des poupées

21 A

Voici Karine, très sportive en maillot de bain vert avec une jupe jaune. Elle a un chapeau jaune aussi. Et voici Boris, très sportif aussi en bermuda bleu avec une chemise bleue et blanche. Il a une veste verte.

Écoute, Karine, où sont mes lunettes noires ? Elles ne sont pas là. Où sont-elles ?

Boris, tu es pénible. Elles sont là – regarde ! Elles sont sur la table.

Et maintenant, voici Karine. Elle porte un pantalon en cuir marron, avec un chemisier rouge pailleté. Elle est sensationnelle. Et voici Boris : il porte un blouson en cuir noir avec un tee-shirt blanc et un jean.

Tu as mes baskets, Karine. Elle ne sont pas dans ma valise !

Voici Karine en jean et un sweat-shirt jaune avec des baskets rouges. Boris porte un survêtement gris avec des baskets blanches et un anorak rouge.

Mais je n'ai pas de chaussures ! Où sont-elles ? Écoute, Karine, mes chaussettes ne sont pas là. Où sont-elles ?

Boris, tes baskets sont là. Regarde-elles sont sous la chaise !

Je ne sais pas, Boris....

Karine est très belle en robe verte. Et voici Boris, très beau en smoking gris avec une chemise blanche et une cravate bleue et grise. Et regardez ses chaussures : elles sont ... ah non ... euh...

... euh, il n'a pas de chaussures.

Karine, mes chaussures sont dans ton sac. Et mes chaussettes sont dans ton sac aussi.

Je suis désolée, Boris....

1. Look through the story and find the French words for these items of clothing.

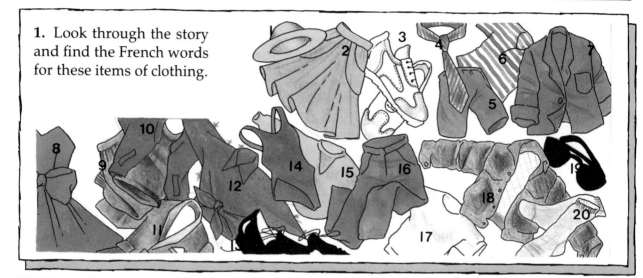

2. Now find the colour that goes with each item of clothing. (Remember that some things have more than one colour and sometimes two things are the same colour.)

a) *jaune*
b *bleu/bleue*
c) *blanc/blanche/blanches*
d) *vert/verte*
e) *noir/noires*
f) *rouge*
g) *gris/grise*

3. Say which of Boris's things are in the places shown by each cross in this picture.

4. Vanessa Paradis was only 14 when her first record became number one of the French charts. But she continued to go to school and look like other French teenagers. She once said in an interview:

– *Je n'ai pas de look particulier . . . J'aime les jeans et les gros blousons . . .*

Which of Karine's clothes do you think Vanessa would like best?

5. Read these descriptions of what Safia, Éric and Nadine have in their wardrobes and in their chests of drawers, and decide which belongs to each of them.

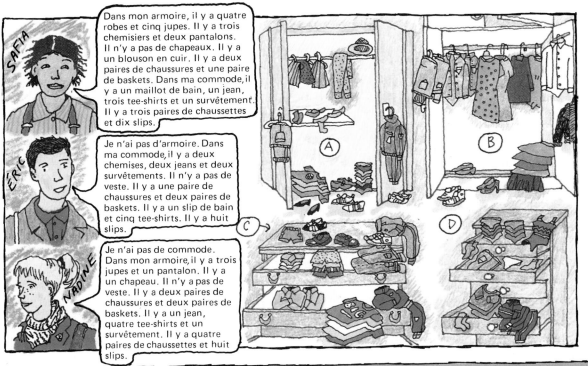

SAFIA

Dans mon armoire, il y a quatre robes et cinq jupes. Il y a trois chemisiers et deux pantalons. Il n'y a pas de chapeaux. Il y a un blouson en cuir. Il y a deux paires de chaussures et une paire de baskets. Dans ma commode, il y a un maillot de bain, un jean, trois tee-shirts et un survêtement. Il y a trois paires de chaussettes et dix slips.

ÉRIC

Je n'ai pas d'armoire. Dans ma commode, il y a deux chemises, deux jeans et deux survêtements. Il n'y a pas de veste. Il y a une paire de chaussures et deux paires de baskets. Il y a un slip de bain et cinq tee-shirts. Il y a huit slips.

NADINE

Je n'ai pas de commode. Dans mon armoire, il y a trois jupes et un pantalon. Il y a un chapeau. Il n'y a pas de veste. Il y a deux paires de chaussures et deux paires de baskets. Il y a un jean, quatre tee-shirts et un survêtement. Il y a quatre paires de chaussettes et huit slips.

6. Now draw and label in your book a picture of each of the items of clothing mentioned above.

7. Work with a partner. Partner A should cover up the list of Safia's clothes on this page. Partner B reads out the items on Safia's list and Partner A writes in next to each picture in his/her exercise book how many of each thing Safia has. Then swap over, and do the same thing with Nadine's clothes. Swap back again, and do Éric's.

8. Now colour in the pictures in your exercise book according to these instructions.

La robe est rouge.
La jupe est verte.
Le chemisier est marron.
Le chapeau est gris.
La veste est bleue.
Le pantalon est noir.

Le survêtement est jaune.
Le blouson est vert.
La chemise est blanche.
Les chaussures sont noires.
Les chaussettes sont grises.
Les baskets sont rouges.

Le maillot de bain est bleu.
Le tee-shirt est vert.
Le slip est blanc.
Le slip de bain est jaune.
Le jean est bleu.

9. Look carefully at the pictures and captions, then work with a partner. Partner A covers up the captions and Partner B chooses one of the pictures and reads the caption. Partner A has to decide which caption Partner B is reading and say either a), b) or c). Then swap over so that the other partner sees the captions this time.

a)

Le chat est sur le lit.

b)

Le chat est sous le lit.

c)

Le chat est dans le lit.

10. Draw and label in your exercise book these things that are in Patrick's bedroom.

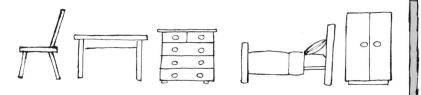

11. Patrick's bedroom is very untidy, and he is going to tell you where lots of his clothes are lying around. As he mentions each piece of clothing, write its name either on top of, under or inside the piece of furniture where it can be found.

12. Draw or trace this picture of Katya's room in your exercise book. Draw in the following things to make the room look more like it usually does!

Sous le lit, il y a un chat. Sur le lit, il y a un ours. Sur la table, il y a des disques. Sous l'armoire, il y a des baskets. Sur la commode, il y a des lunettes et une montre. Dans l'armoire, il y a des robes. Dans la commode, il y a des chaussettes.

Without looking at your drawing of Katya's room, try to remember as many objects as possible.

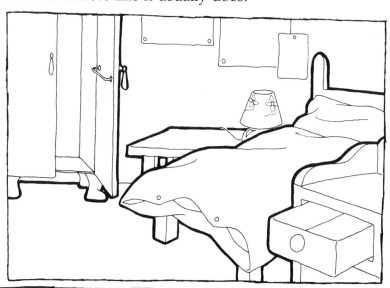

13. Now you're going to hear about a room of a very different kind, but what you hear won't all be true. As you listen to the tape, compare what Madame Dracula says with the picture and note down in your exercise book three things Madame Dracula says that aren't true.

Bravo!

OBJECTIFS ATTEINTS

Now you can . . .

. . . say what clothes there are in your wardrobe
Il y a . . .

. . . say what is not there
Il n'y a pas de . . .

. . . say where things are
Tes lunettes sont dans/sur/sous . . .

. . . say what colour something is
J'ai un pantalon bleu (rouge, etc).

Talking about the position of people and things

● All languages have ways of showing the position of people or things in relation to other people or things. In English and in French this is done by a set of words like 'in' (*dans* in French), 'on' (*sur* in French), 'under' (*sous* in French) and many others. These words are called **prepositions**.

14. Can you think of any more prepositions in English? (Here are a few to start you off: 'across', 'over', 'inside' . . .)

15. Now see how many pairs of opposites there are, for example, 'over'/'under'. Write a poem in which each line begins with a preposition. You could write about a land very far away, or a secret that was hidden. Here are some song and book titles that might help you: 'Over the Rainbow', 'Under the Volcano', 'Behind the Lines'.

16. There are other words or expressions that you can use to talk about position, for instance, 'move', 'climb', 'disappear', etc. Try this exercise with a partner. Find a photograph that you can tell a story about (from a family album, or from a newspaper). Swap photos with your partner, and write what was happening in it. Check with your partner to see if you guessed right, then underline any words or expressions that are to do with describing where people or things are.

17. Sometimes we use prepositions differently in different languages. In English, we'd say: "In the photo there is . . ." but a French speaker would say, *Sur la photo* . . . Look back at some of the language you've already learned and think how a French speaker would say:
a) "I live in Paris."
b) "On Friday."
c) "In the morning."
(Be careful – these are trick questions!)

TES OBJECTIFS

In this unit, you will learn how to . . .

. . . offer a choice of items to eat or drink

. . . choose something to eat or drink

. . . accept or reject an offer of food

. . . say what is and isn't available

. . . ask if someone wants more of something

. . . show your appreciation of food

22 A *Le petit déjeuner*

1. Make two lists in your exercise book, one for what Katya has for breakfast and one for what Djamel has. Begin the lists with the words *Katya prend . . .* and *Djamel prend. . . .* These are the items that you will need to choose from:

du café	*des biscottes*	*du beurre*
du chocolat	*du pain*	*de la confiture*

2. Write out in your exercise book the names of the items on Madame Tedjini's breakfast tray.

3. Design your own ideal breakfast tray, and draw and label all the items on it in your exercise book.

A

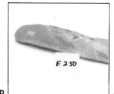

B

C

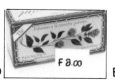

D

E

F

G

H

I

J

4. Can you put these groceries away into the right place?

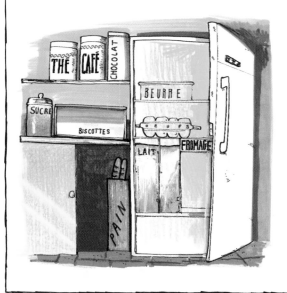

5. Work with a partner, so that only one of you sees the price labels on the groceries. The other one asks these questions:

a) *C'est combien, le sucre?*
b) *C'est combien, le café?*
c) *C'est combien, le thé?*
d) *C'est combien, le beurre?*
e) *C'est combien, le lait?*
f) *C'est combien, les œufs?*
g) *C'est combien, le pain?*
h) *C'est combien, les biscottes?*
i) *C'est combien, le fromage?*
j) *C'est combien, le chocolat?*

Le déjeuner

Sarah stayed for school lunch for the first time today, and Jean explained to her all the things that were available.

6. What do you think Sarah chooses? Here are some clues:

Elle ne mange pas de viande. Elle aime le poisson. Elle aime les pâtisseries.

Bon. Comme entrée, il y a du pâté, des tomates ou des sardines. Comme plat principal, il y a du bifteck, du poulet ou des oeufs. Et il y a des frites et de la salade. Comme dessert, il y a du fromage, de la tarte aux pommes, des yaourts ou des fruits.

7. Here are some more dishes from Raymond's fridge. What would you say if you were offering them to Ted, and what would his answer be? (Remember that he adores all food.) Write down your answers in your exercise book.

8. Listen to the tape and decide which fridge belongs to which dwarf.

1   2   3   4   5   6   7

9. Work with a partner. Each of you secretly choose one of the fridges, then try and guess what is in the other's fridge by asking *Il y a . . .?* (or *Est-ce qu'il y a . . .?*). Answer *Oui, il y a du/de la/des/de l' . . .*, or *Non, il n'y a pas de . . .* When you have found out which of the seven dwarves the other is supposed to be, say *Tu es . . .* and the name. Then start again with two more fridges.

Bravo!

OBJECTIFS ATTEINTS

10. Le dîner

Patrick has been invited to the restaurant that Sophie's grandparents (Monsieur and Madame Thireau) run. Make a note of what each of the four people have to eat and drink.

Now you can . . .

. . . offer a choice of items to eat or drink

Tu prends/Tu veux du/de la/ de l'/des . . .?

. . . choose something to eat or drink

Je prends du/de la/de l'/des . . .

. . . accept or reject an offer of food

Oui, s'il te (vous) plaît, je veux bien. Je ne veux pas de . . ./Non, merci.

. . . ask if someone wants more of something

Encore du/de la/de l'/des . . .?

. . . show your appreciation of food

C'est délicieux./C'est très bon.

Talking about an unknown amount of something

Asking for some chips, some chicken, some lemonade or even some water is more complicated in French than in English because there are four different ways of saying 'some'.

● If there's more than one thing (for example, *frites*, *hamburgers*) you use *des*.

● If there's one thing and it begins with a vowel or (sometimes) 'h' use *de l'* (as in *de l'eau*, *de l'Orangina*).
● If there's one thing and it's a feminine word (that is, a word that can have *la* or *une* in front of it) use *de la* (for example, *de la limonade*, *de la soupe*).
● If there's one thing and it's a masculine word (that is, a word that can have *le* or *un* in front of it) use *du* (as in *du poulet*, *du bifteck*).

11. Look at the groceries in this bag: *du sucre*; *du café*; *du chocolat*. Draw three other bags labelled *de la*, *des* and *de l'* and list the groceries you would put in each one.

But what if the supermarket runs out of groceries?

In a negative sentence (for example, *Il n'y a pas de . . .*, *Je n'ai pas de . . .*, *Elle ne mange pas de . . .*) the words for 'some', like *du*, *de la*, *de l'* and *des*, all turn into *de*.

12. Make some signs for your school canteen to say what's not available. For example, *Il n'y a pas de champagne*.

13. This advert says that to make Saint-Nectaire cheese, you need time (*du temps*) and a little genius (*un peu de génie*). Try and decide what the third vital ingredient is.

SAINT-NECTAIRE
CANTOREL

AVEC DU LAIT, DU TEMPS,
ET UN PEU DE GÉNIE

TES OBJECTIFS

In this unit, you will learn how to . . .

. . . talk and ask about things that you and other people do at home

. . . give more details about the position of people and objects

 1. Listen to Patrick reading this story to his younger brother Fabien, and then see if you can do the exercises that Fabien has to do on the next page.

| La mère de Pierre | Le père de Pierre | La grand-mère de Pierre | Le frère de Pierre |

Réponds:

(i) Qui fait la vaisselle?
(ii) Qui fait ses devoirs?
(iii) Qui fait un jeu vidéo?
(iv) Qui fait le lit?
(v) Qui boit de la limonade?

Complète les phrases:

(i) On fait la vaisselle . . .   dans la chambre.
(ii) On mange . . .   dans la cuisine.
(iii) On fait des jeux vidéo . . .   dans le jardin.
(iv) On fait ses devoirs . . .   dans le salon.
(v) On fait le lit . . .   dans la salle à manger.
(vi) On boit de la limonade . . .

2. Work with a partner. Choose to be one of the four people in the story and write down that person's name, for example, *La grand-mère de Pierre*. Then take it in turns with your partner to guess who each other is by asking what he/she is doing. For example, *Tu fais la vaisselle?* The first person to get *Oui* as an answer is the winner. Then choose two different people and start again.

3. Now Fabien is telling Patrick a story with the aid of his dolls' house. Listen, and see if you can work out who is doing what. . . .

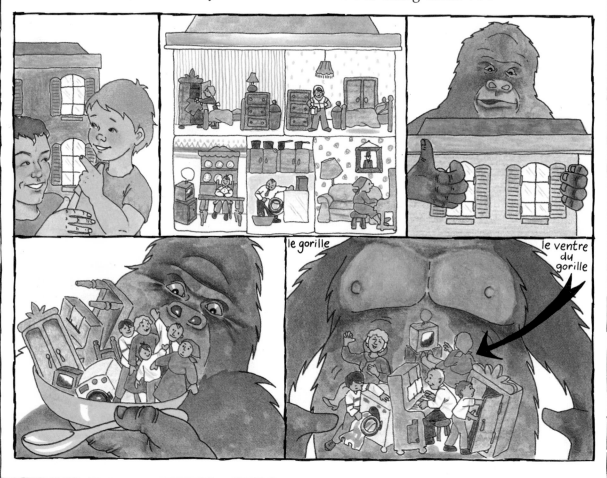

le gorille

le ventre du gorille

4. Decide whether these sentences about what people are doing before the gorilla arrives are true or false. *C'est vrai ou c'est faux?* Write the answers in your exercise book.

a) *La mère fait la vaisselle.*
b) *Le père fait la lessive.*
c) *Le frère de Pierre écoute un walkman.*
d) *La grand-mère de Pierre regarde la télévision.*
e) *Pierre range ses affaires.*

5. Write out in your exercise book what each person is doing inside the gorilla's stomach.

6. Here are some children's pictures showing what they and their grandmothers do every day. Can you decide which picture goes with which caption?

Ma journée

1. Je fais mon lit.
2. Je travaille en classe.
3. Je mange de la soupe.
4. Je range mes affaires.
5. Je fais mes devoirs.
6. Je fais la vaisselle.

La journée de ma grand-mère

1. Elle écoute son walkman.
2. Elle regarde la télévision.
3. Elle mange des hamburgers.
4. Elle fait des jeux vidéo.
5. Elle joue de la guitare.
6. Elle danse sur la table.

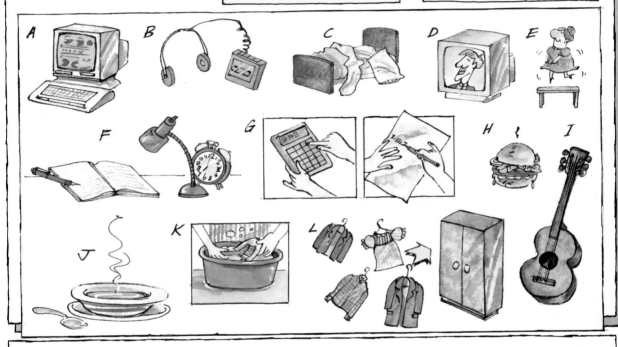

7. Listen to Sophie, Patrick and Jean talking about how often they do all these activities. Draw three columns in your exercise book. The first one (labelled *Tous les jours*) is for the things they do every day, the second one (labelled *Quelquefois*) is for things they do sometimes and the third one (*Jamais*) is for things they never do. For each activity write the corresponding letter and the name of the person speaking into one of the three columns.

8. Work with a partner. Write out a list of three things you do every day, for instance *Je fais mon lit tous les jours*, and then three things you do sometimes, for instance *Je mange quelquefois des hamburgers*. Prepare a similar list for what you think your partner does (*Il/Elle fait . . ., Il/Elle joue . . .*), and finally compare your lists with your partner's own lists.

9. *Complète le travail de Patrick.* Finish off adding the captions to Patrick's project about his family. Write out the remaining captions in your exercise book.

Voici mon frère Fabien. Il est derrière le chien.

Voici ma soeur. Elle est derrière un arbre.

Voici ma mère. Elle est devant la tour Eiffel.

Voici mes frères. Ils sont derrière une statue, à Paris.

C'est moi. Là, j'ai trois ans. Je suis devant la maison de ma grand-mère.

C'est mon père devant l'usine.

1

C'est mon frère Michel . . .

2

C'est moi . . .

3

Voici mes cousins . . .

10. *Maintenant complète les phrases.* The captions to go with these pictures from other people's projects are incomplete. Write out the full captions in your exercise book.

Bravo!

OBJECTIFS ATTEINTS

Now you can . . .

. . . talk and ask about things that you and other people do at home

> *Je fais la vaisselle.*
> *Tu fais la vaisselle?*
> *Il/Elle fait la vaisselle.*
> *On fait la vaisselle.*

. . . give more details about the position of people and objects

> *Je suis devant/derrière . . .*
> *Où es-tu?*

Learning language patterns

It's not fair! Just when I'd learned the pattern for <u>aimer</u> and <u>détester</u>, we've started to have spelling tests on verbs that have a different pattern – and there are some verbs that just follow their own pattern...

Well, let's start by trying to cheer you up! I'll mime some verbs that follow the <u>détester</u> pattern and you guess what they are, o.k.?

danser
travailler
manger
regarder
jouer
écouter

11. Can you guess the words?

The *-re* verbs are not so bad: at least, they have their own pattern.

j'attends
tu attends
il / elle attend
nous attendons
vous attendez
ils / elles attendent

You have to be careful with the spelling of *manger* and *ranger*, though.

Nous mangeons
Nous rangeons

12. Try and design a similar page, but use *descendre* as an example of an *-re* verb.

Sarah: It's the ones that follow their own pattern that I don't like.

Mother: But all languages have irregular verbs, and children find them difficult even in their own language. You used to say 'I swimmed' and 'I runned' when you were small.

13. See if you can think of any more irregular verbs in English that children often get wrong. Why do you think they make these mistakes?

14. Sarah had to do a test at school. Can you help her?

Je fais
Tu fais ?
Il ..... ?

Je veux ?
Tu ..... ?
Elle veut

Je ...... ?
Tu prends
On prend

Unité 24

TES OBJECTIFS

In this unit, you will learn how to . . .
. . . talk about the weather
. . . say what you and your friends do after school
. . . talk about what friends and neighbours do every day

 1. *Écoute: Quel jour on est?* Listen to the tape and from what is said about the weather, work out what day it is.

2. *Écoute: Où sont-ils?* Listen to the tape and look carefully at these photographs. Work out where each person is from the weather they are describing.

Paris en automne

Rouen au printemps

Dans les Alpes en hiver

Les Arcs en hiver

Les Gorges du Tarn au printemps

Cannes en été

Paris en automne

3. *Écris des cartes postales.* Now write a postcard from each of the places on the photos.

30000 **NIMES** *(Gard)*
Arènes construites peu avant l'ère chrétienne, mesurent 137 m sur 100 m et pouvaient contenir 21.000 spectateurs

Salut Laurent

Il fait du brouillard à Nîmes.

Damien

Laurent Bougard
7 boulevard St-Germain

75007 Paris

La sortie de l'école

What Katya and her friends do after school depends on the weather. Here she tells you some of the things that they do.

Quand il fait beau . . .

a) *on fait du vélo . . .*   b) *on joue au foot . . .*   c) *on parle avec les copains devant l'école . . .*   d) *on fait les magasins.*

Quand il fait mauvais . . .

a) *on rentre . . .*   b) *on regarde la télé à la maison . . .*   c) *on joue au babyfoot avec les copains dans un café . . .*   d) *on joue au flipper.*

4. Now listen to three of Katya's friends saying whether they do the things that she has already mentioned. Write out a list in your exercise book of all the activities Katya has mentioned and for each person put *Oui* or *Non* against the activity.

5. Now look at Katya's list again and write down in your exercise book the things that you do and the things you don't do after school. Then ask your partner, for example, *Quand il fait beau, tu fais du vélo?* and write down what he/she does and doesn't do.

Daniel Lagarde est inspecteur de police. Il est dans un café et il observe Monsieur et Madame Deschamps.

Monsieur et Madame Deschamps quittent la maison à sept heures et demie...Ils montent dans la voiture... Ils font un tour en voiture.

Ils rentrent à dix-huit heures... Madame Deschamps entre dans la maison. Monsieur Deschamps n'entre pas dans la maison tout de suite... il traverse la rue... il entre au tabac. Il passe deux minutes dans le tabac. Il quitte le tabac... Il entre dans la maison.

Madame Vincent quitte la maison à sept heures et demie... Elle traverse la rue... Elle entre dans la boulangerie... Elle quitte la boulangerie... retraverse la rue et rentre chez elle. Elle quitte la maison avec ses trois enfants à huit heures dix... Ils traversent la rue... Les enfants montent dans l'autobus devant la boulangerie... Madame Vincent ne monte pas dans l'autobus avec les enfants. Elle retraverse la rue... Elle monte dans sa voiture.

Elle rentre à dix-sept heures cinq... Les enfants rentrent à dix-sept heures quinze... Ils n'entrent pas dans la maison tout de suite. Ils font des courses ?...Non...Ils parlent avec des copains devant la maison... Ils entrent dans la maison à dix-huit heures...

6. Is this diagram an accurate account of the movements of Monsieur and Madame Deschamps?

7. Now draw quite a big diagram of the street in your exercise book and draw in arrows to show the movements of the Vincent family.

 24 E

8. Listen to what they can hear, and see if you agree with Fabrice or his wife . . .

Fabrice et sa femme entendent les voisins....

Mais non! Ils n'écoutent pas la radio. Ils chantent.

C'est les Jamin. Ils écoutent la radio.

Maintenant ils font la vaisselle.

Mais non! Ils ne font pas la vaisselle. Ils préparent le dîner.

Aaaooooo!!

Ça, c'est le chien des Jamin. Il chante.

Non, le chien ne chante pas. Les enfants ont un synthétiseur. Ils jouent du synthétiseur.

Aïee!!

C'est Madame Jamin! Elle saute par la fenêtre!

Non, Madame Jamin ne saute pas par la fenêtre. C'est Monsieur Jamin. Il gare la voiture.

9. This man is getting worked up about the youth of today. . .

> Ils ne travaillent pas en classe, ils regardent par la fenêtre. Ils ne font pas leurs devoirs, ils font des jeux vidéo. Ils ne jouent pas au rugby, ils jouent au flipper. Ils ne portent pas de chaussures, ils portent des baskets. Ils ne mangent pas de bifteck, ils mangent des hamburgers. Le soir, ils ne rentrent pas directement à la maison, ils traînent dans les cafés.

He is certainly not right about François-Xavier and Rodolphe . . . Write out the correct statements in your exercise book. For example, *Ils ne regardent pas par la fenêtre, ils travaillent en classe.*

– The boys' mother is so upset that she can't finish the questions she wanted to ask them, such as *Vous travaillez en classe, mes enfants, ou vous regardez par la fenêtre?* . . . Can you complete them for her?

– The boys decide to set the record straight by writing to the man on television. Can you finish off their letter? *Monsieur, nous sommes deux lycéens. Nous travaillons beaucoup. . .*

Bravo! OBJECTIFS ATTEINTS

Now you can . . .

. . . talk about the weather
> *Il fait beau./Il pleut./Il fait du vent.*

. . . say what you and your friends do after school
> *On joue au flipper.*
> *On regarde la télévision.*

. . . talk about what friends and neighbours do every day
> *Ils rentrent à six heures.*
> *Ils promènent le chien.*

POINT LANGUE

Spelling in French

> Why do we have to do so many *dictées* at school? We have them practically every day.

> It's because French has so many silent letters. Like 's' when it's on the end of a word.

Lee: But if you don't sound the 's' on the end of a word, how can you tell if it's plural or not? I mean if there's no difference between *chat* and *chats*, how do you know how many there are? There might be about fifty, all leaping through your window, and . . .

Mother: Lee, think about it. Look at these two pictures. Now, tell me which picture I'm talking about.

- *Voici mon chat.*
- *Voici mes chats.*
- *C'est le chat.*
- *C'est les chats.*
- *Il y a un chat.*
- *Il y a des chats.*

Mother: That's right. French just doesn't work like English when it comes to matching letters up with sounds so don't try and sound the word out as if it was an English word. Try and remember how it sounded when you heard your teacher say it. Here are a few for you to practise on. How many of the words that I've underlined in each of these groups sound exactly the same as each other?

Lee: Yes, I see what you mean. But it's not just the 's' on the ends of words that causes trouble. You don't pronounce 't' at the end either, or 'd' or 'x', except in a few words.

Je veux un sandwich
Tu veux un sandwich
Elle veut un sandwich

Je regarde la télé.
Tu regardes la télé.
Il regarde la télé.
Ils regardent la télé.

Je fais la vaisselle.
Tu fais la vaisselle.
On fait la vaisselle.

Je prends un café.
Tu prends un café.
Elle prend un café.

Play this game with a partner. Throw the dice to determine what the weather is. If you throw first, your partner will ask _Quel temps fait-il?_ and you must answer according to the number thrown. If you throw a six, you would say _Il fait du vent_. Your partner will then ask you whether you have the appropriate object, for example, _Tu as un cerf-volant?_ Throw the dice again to decide which room of the house you're in. Move the counter to that room and tell your partner where you are, for example, _Je suis dans la cuisine_. If that room contains the object that you need then say _Oui_. That object is now yours and cannot be won by your partner. If you do not land in the right room say _Non_ and your partner will go on to throw the dice to find out what the weather is. The game ends when all the objects are won.

For a more complicated game, when you land in a room where your object is you can only have the object once you have thrown the dice a third time to locate exactly where it is.
If you throw :

- ☐ a one or a two, say the object is _sur la table_
- ☐ a three, say the object is _sous le lit_
- ☐ a four, say the object is _dans la commode_

- ☐ a five, say the object is _sous la table_
- ☐ a six, say the object is _dans l'armoire_

Try these listening activities!

 25 B **1.** Listen to the weather report and plan your trip through France, starting at Boulogne and going only through the towns where the weather is good.

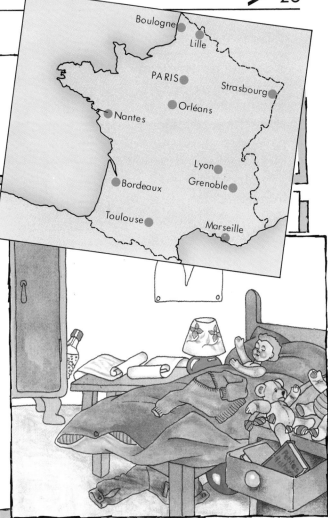

 25 C **2.** This is a picture of Katya's room as she finds it after her brother and sister have been playing in it. But listen to her: does she get things right? Copy out all the items in Katya's bedroom: put a tick by the things which are where she says they are, and a cross by the others.

une veste en cuir　　*deux ours*
des posters　　　　　*un ballon*
un pull-over　　　　　*des bonbons*
des livres　　　　　　*une poupée*
de la limonade

 25 D **3.** One of Patrick's cousins, Richard, is coming to stay from Canada. The family have not seen Richard since he was small, and Patrick's mother is phoning Richard's mother to find out what he likes doing. She has drawn up a list of possible activities and food. Copy out the list into your exercise book and cross off the ones that he won't want to do or eat.

télé
jeux vidéo
vélo
guitare
football
hamburgers
frites
café
chocolat
tartines

Try these writing activities!

4. Write (i) about your own room, (ii) about an imaginary room that you would like to have.

5. Write about what you do in your free time when the weather's good and when it's bad.

Try these reading activities!

6. Sophie is helping out in her grandparents' restaurant. She has to serve three customers who have each chosen one of these menus. Write down in your exercise book the numbers of the dishes that each person has.

madame Giros	monsieur Giros	monsieur Boyer
30 francs	35 francs	40 francs
tomates	soupe	pâté
hamburger	poulet	bifteck
frites	petits pois	frites
fromage	tarte aux pommes	salade
		fromage
		fruits

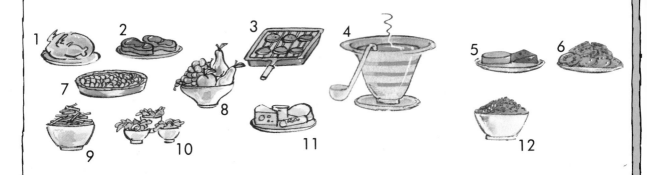

7. A teenage magazine is trying to find out what are the most popular free-time activities amongst its readers. Here is some of the information they have been sent by readers. Copy out the names of the four teenagers (Marie-France, Jean-Jacques, Hélène, Benjamin) and add the numbers corresponding to the activities they like.

Paris, le 5 mai

Je m'appelle Marie-France. J'ai treize ans. Je fais des jeux vidéo. Je fais du vélo. J'écoute mon walkman. Et je danse! Salut!

Marie-France

Marseille, le 18 mai

Je m'appelle Jean-Jacques. J'ai douze ans. Je joue au foot et je joue au baby-foot. Je fais du vélo et je fais des jeux vidéo. Salut!

Jean-Jacques

20.5.88

Je m'appelle Hélène. J'ai treize ans. Je chante, je danse, j'écoute de la musique et je joue de la guitare. Salut! Hélène.

Nevers, le 3 mai 1988

Je m'appelle Benjamin. J'ai douze ans. Je fais des jeux vidéo. Je regarde la télé et je joue au baby-foot. Salut!

Benjamin.

TES OBJECTIFS

In this unit, you will learn how to . . .

. . . say how you feel or someone else feels

. . . ask someone how they feel

. . . offer some simple advice or a remedy
to someone according to how they feel

1. Who is saying what? Match up the picture with the problem . . .

2. Work with a partner. Partner A points at one of the eight pictures above and asks: *Qu'est-ce qu'il/elle a?* Partner B says what is wrong with him/her. For example, *Il/Elle a mal . . .* When you've done this three times, change over so that Partner B asks the questions.

26 B   *Le hibou et le chat*

3. What would the cat like? Look at how she feels in each picture below and for each statement say which item would make her feel better.

4. Find the phrases in the story that mean the following and write them down in your exercise book.

a) That's enough!   b) I'm fed up!   c) What a pity!

Je n'ai pas faim!

 5. Is Sophie's grandmother a little over-protective? Listen to the conversations Sophie has with her *mamie* and decide which of the four items (*pull-over*, *limonade*, *sandwich* and *glace*) she accepts or turns down.

6. Listen to what is wrong with these people. Write down their names in your exercise book. Listen to them again and indicate beside each name what advice each person is given.

A

Va à l'hôpital.

B

Va à la pharmacie.

C

Va chez le docteur.

D
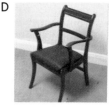
Assieds-toi.

E

Achète des pastilles.

F
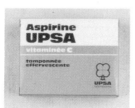
Prends de l'aspirine.

G

Va au lit.

H

Prends un café.

7. Katya's little sister has received a doll-making kit. There should be ten items included in it. She is checking the parts but realises there is one item missing. Can you work out what it is?

les yeux
les cheveux
la bouche
le corps
les mains
les jambes
les pieds
les bras
le nez
la tête

> *Voici ma poupée. Eh bien...*
> *il y a une tête, un nez,*
> *les yeux, les cheveux, les bras,*
> *le corps, les jambes,*
> *les pieds, les mains. Mais*
> *elle n'a pas de ...*

Bravo! OBJECTIFS ATTEINTS

Now you can . . .

. . . say how you feel or someone else feels
J'ai/Il/Elle a soif/faim/mal à . . .
Je suis fatigué(e)/de mauvaise humeur.

. . . ask someone how they feel
Qu'est-ce que tu as?/Tu as chaud?/Tu es fatigué(e)?

. . . offer some simple advice or a remedy
Va chez le docteur./Prends de l'aspirine./Achète des pastilles./Assieds-toi.

Spotting similarities with other languages

"You've probably heard of me, Julius Caesar, and you might have heard of Latin, the language we used in the Roman Empire. I wonder how many of you will learn Latin in the next few years."

"It's true that not many people today use Latin as it was originally spoken – but many people speak languages that have developed from Latin. Have a quick look at the Roman Empire a few years after I took over . . ."

"Gradually we took over the areas you now call Spain and France and even that cold, damp, northern territory you call Britain."

"When our soldiers invaded, the languages that people used in those countries became less widely used, and Latin took over as the official language."

Non comprehendo = I don't understand

"The Latin used in Italy, Spain and France gradually changed and two thousand years later has become Italian, Spanish and French, but there are still a lot of similarities between the languages. In Britain, things were a bit more complicated because it was invaded by many other people, too, so English is a mixture of far more things. But there is a lot of Latin in the English language. Take the Latin word for foot, *pes/pedes* and in English you have: 'pedestrian', 'pedal', 'pedestal', 'biped'. Do you know what all these mean?"

8. Once you know one language, other languages become easier, even if you haven't learned them. Listen to these people mentioning five different parts of the body in Spanish and try to work out what they mean.

English	Latin	French	Italian
arm	*bracchium*	*bras*	*braccio*
stomach	*stomachus*	*ventre**	*stomaco*
foot	*pes/pedes*	*pied*	*piede*
nose	*nasus*	*nez*	*naso*
hand	*manus*	*main*	*mano*

*the word *estomac* is also used in French

TES OBJECTIFS   In this unit, you will learn how to . . .

. . . say where you're going

. . . ask someone where they're going

. . . invite someone to go with you

. . . accept or turn down an invitation to go somewhere

 27 A *Monsieur Duforge est chauffeur de taxi. Sa vie est calme. Trop calme. Aujourd'hui il s'ennuie . . .*

27 B **1.** Listen again to the driver saying where he is going. Match up one statement from the story with each of these pictures.

Le week-end de Jean

2. Where is Jean off to? Write in your exercise book where he says he is going.

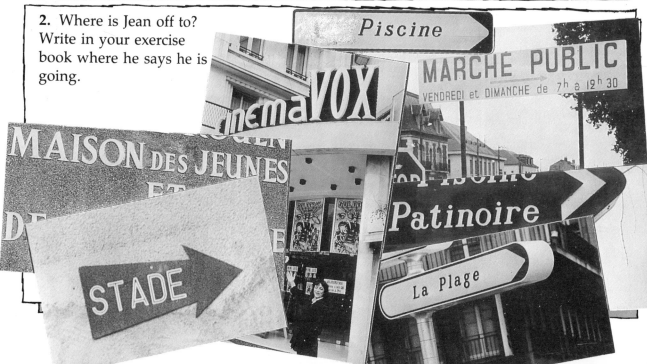

27 D *Où allez-vous?*

3. A survey is taking place about where motorists are going to. Make a list of all the places marked on the map. Listen to the interviews and put a tick by each place as you hear it mentioned. What is the most popular destination today?

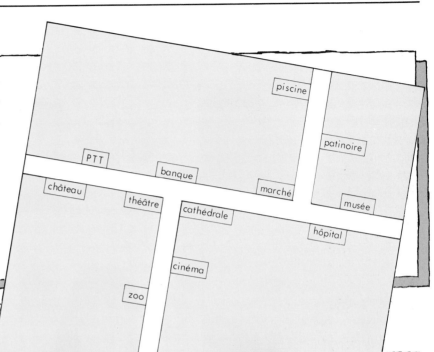

 27 E *À la plage*

 4. Work with a partner. Take it in turns to invite and accept invitations to go to these places.

Allô. Oui, c'est Aurélie Ah! bonjour, François.

Au musée?...

Allô. Céline? Salut!...

Salut, Luc. Quoi? À la piscine à deux heures?...

Béatrice? Tiens! Ça va?...

Allô. Qui? Julien? Oui...

5. How many lies do you think Aurélie tells? Look back at activity 4., and this time turn down your partner's invitations with excuses similar to Aurélie's.

Bravo!
OBJECTIFS ATTEINTS

Now you can . . .

. . . say where you're going	*Je vais à la plage.* *Je vais au marché.*
. . . ask someone where they are going	*Où vas-tu?* *Où allez-vous?*
. . . invite someone to go with you	*Tu viens?*
. . . accept an invitation	*D'accord./Je veux bien.*
. . . turn down an invitation	*Je n'ai pas envie.* *Je n'ai pas le temps.* *Je n'ai pas d'argent.* *J'ai trop de devoirs.*

Body language

● The words a person uses and the actual way they say them both convey messages. When you're listening on the telephone, those are the only clues that can tell you what the other person feels about what they're saying.

● But if you're looking at someone, it's quite different. There are a lot of other clues that come from what is called **body language**. The way we sit or stand, what we do with our hands, the expression on our faces – all of these can convey messages to other people. Sometimes, they even give away things we would rather not say. For example, our hands may tremble when we're nervous.

Look at these four back views.

Even with the sound turned off on the television you'd have no difficulty in reading the messages here.

6. Work with a partner, take two of these pictures each and describe in as much detail as you can what expressions each of those people would have on their faces. How might their hands also be adding to the message in each case?

7. Still working with a partner, try and demonstrate different ways of sitting (for example, watching an exciting sporting event, waiting for a train that is two hours late or in a dentist's waiting room). Don't tell your partner what the situation is and don't use words or the expression on your face to give clues.

8. Now think of six different situations in which a person might say *non!* in a particular way. Demonstrate them with facial expressions and body movements and get others to guess what they are.

9. Demonstrate how the speaker might look in each of these cases using body language but not saying the words:

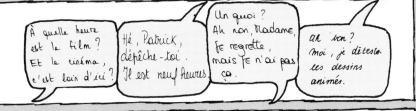

● Now that you know about body language, look out for it: it's all around you.

Unite 28

TES OBJECTIFS

In this unit, you will learn how to . . .

. . . ask permission to do something

. . . check whether it's all right to do something

. . . ask why and understand reasons for doing/not doing something

La visite

1. Match each of these pictures with the appropriate question on the tape.

A   B   C

Qu'est-ce qu'on peut faire?

2. All the speech bubbles are in the wrong place. Match each of these signs with the appropriate speech bubble.

1
CHIENS INTERDITS

2 SORTIE DE GARAGE DÉFENSE DE STATIONNER

3 ENTREE DU ZOO

4 DEFENSE DE FUMER

A *On peut téléphoner ici.*

B *On ne peut pas entrer avec un chien.*

C *On ne peut pas fumer ici.*

D *On peut traverser la rue maintenant.*

5 Camping SHELL BERRE

6

7 ABRI TELEPHONE

8

E *On ne peut pas traverser la rue.*

F *On peut entrer par ici.*

G *On peut camper ici.*

H *On ne peut pas stationner ici.*

Enquête

3. *Dans ton école, est-ce qu'on peut . . .?* Copy this grid into your exercise book and say whether you can/can't/only sometimes do each of the five things in your school.

Est-ce qu'on peut . . .	oui	non	quelquefois
1. *bavarder en classe?*			
2. *porter un jean?*			
3. *avoir des cheveux rouges, bleus ou verts?*			
4. *manger en classe?*			
5. *fumer dans la cour?*	*Copie cette grille dans ton cahier.*		

Bonjour, tu veux un café?

Non, merci.

Pourquoi?

Parce que j'ai une limonade.

Tu veux un gâteau?

Non, merci.

Pourquoi?

Parce que je n'ai pas faim.

Tu veux une cigarette?

Non, je ne veux pas de cigarette.

Pourquoi?

Parce que je ne fume pas.

Tu veux aller au cinéma?

Non, je ne veux pas aller au cinéma.

Pourquoi? Tu n'aimes pas le cinéma?

Écoute... Je n'ai pas faim, je n'ai pas soif, je ne veux pas de cigarette. J'aime bien le cinéma, mais je déteste les garçons comme toi!

Pourquoi?

4. Match up each of the following questions with an appropriate response.

Les questions:
1. *Tu ne veux pas de café? Pourquoi?*
2. *Tu ne veux pas de gâteau? Pourquoi?*
3. *Tu ne veux pas de cigarette? Pourquoi?*
4. *Tu ne veux pas aller au cinéma? Pourquoi?*

Les réponses:
A *Parce que je n'ai pas faim.*
B *Parce que je déteste les cigarettes.*
C *Parce que je n'aime pas les films.*
D *Parce que je n'ai pas soif.*

5. Work with a partner. Your partner offers you something or invites you somewhere, as illustrated here (A, B or C). Each time you must give a reason for rejecting the offer or invitation. Now change over and work from the second group of illustrations (D, E or F) so that your partner rejects your offers.

28 D **6.** Katya, Jean, Sophie, Patrick and Sarah all want to go to the school disco on Saturday night. Listen to each of them asking for permission to go. Copy this grid into your exercise book. Who can go and on what condition? Who can't go and why?

	oui	condition	non	pourquoi
Katya				
Jean		*Copie cette grille dans ton cahier.*		
Sophie				
Patrick				
Sarah				

7. Katya had to write 100 lines the other day at school as a punishment. Read it carefully and work out why she was punished.

Je ne dois pas bavarder et je ne dois pas manger en classe.
Je ne dois pas bavarder et je ne dois pas manger en classe.
Je ne dois pas bavarder et je ne dois pas manger en classe.
Je ne dois pas bavarder et je ne dois pas manger en classe.
Je ne dois pas bavarder et je ne dois pas manger en classe.
Je ne dois pas bavarder et je ne dois pas manger en classe.
Je ne dois pas bavarder et je ne dois pas manger en classe.
Je ne dois pas bavarder et je ne dois pas manger en classe.

Bravo!

OBJECTIFS ATTEINTS

Now you can . . .

. . . ask permission to do something   *Est-ce que je peux?*

. . . check whether it's all right to do something
                                           Est-ce qu'on peut?

. . . ask why   *Pourquoi?*

. . . understand reason   *Parce que tu dois . . .*

Infinitives

Hamlet has met a beautiful woman who has been staying with her aunt nearby. Her holidays are now at an end. . . .

"I beg you to stay."

"I hate to leave."

"I'd like to take you in my arms once more. . . ."

"I have to get on the train now. Goodbye, Hamlet."

"Let's promise to write every day."

"To be or not to be? That is the question."

"Hamlet, your tea's ready. Are you going to come down?"

When verbs have the word 'to' in front of them, like 'to eat', 'to leave' or 'to be', this is called an **infinitive**.

8. Look back at this story and make a list of all the verbs that are in the infinitive.

● In French, there isn't a separate word to show that a verb is in the infinitive. You have to look at the ending of a verb. If a verb ends with *-er, -ir, -re,* or *-oir*, it is probably an infinitive.
Here are some examples:
aller = to go   *choisir* = to choose   *attendre* = to wait   *pouvoir* = to be able to

This is the way words are listed in dictionaries.

9. Look back at the stories in this unit. Make a list of all the French words in the infinitive that you can find.

Unité 29

TES OBJECTIFS   In this unit, you will learn how to . . .

. . . explain where something is
. . . say what you would like to do
. . . arrange where and when to meet
. . . say what you are going to wear or take
. . . say what you've found, lost or left behind

---

 29 A *Rendez-vous à la gare*

Je déteste ma femme. Elle est cruelle...

Je déteste mon mari. Il est sévère...

Viens à Paris avec moi. Il y a un train à 22 heures 15.

D'accord. Mais où est la gare?

Eh bien, tu quittes le château. Il y a un hôtel en face du château... Il y a un café à côté de l'hôtel...

Devant le café, il y a un arrêt d'autobus. Prends l'autobus et descends à la gare.

À la gare, il y a un buffet. Attends-moi près du buffet. Tu comprends?

BUFFET

Attention! Le train à destination de Paris...

Ce film est vraiment bête. Je suis fatiguée. Je vais au lit.

---

 29 B

1. Help the heroine sort out what she's got to do. Listen to the tape and match the thought bubbles with what she says.

A GARE SNCF

B BUFFET

C Café

Jean, Katya, Patrick, Sarah et Sophie vont passer une journée à Paris. Mais il y a beaucoup de décisions à prendre.

Katya: *Je voudrais aller au Centre Pompidou.*

Jean: *Oui, moi aussi.*

Sarah: *Moi, je voudrais voir la tour Eiffel et faire une promenade en bateau-mouche.*

Sophie: *Patrick et moi, nous voulons aller à la Cité de la Villette.*

Sarah: *Qu'est-ce que c'est?*

Patrick: *Il y a des trucs scientifiques. C'est vraiment intéressant!*

Katya: *Et je voudrais aller dans les grands magasins.*

Sophie: *Tu peux aller dans les magasins à Nantes!*

Katya: *Oui, c'est vrai! Mais je voudrais aller au Marché aux Puces . . .*

Jean: *Oui, ça m'intéresse aussi . . . Mais c'est assez loin du centre.*

Sophie: *J'ai une idée . . . On peut commencer par le Centre Pompidou ou la Cité de la Villette. L'après-midi, Katya peut aller au Marché aux Puces avec toi. Et Patrick, Sarah et moi pouvons aller à la tour Eiffel.*

Jean: *Et vous pouvez prendre un bateau-mouche à côté de la tour Eiffel.*

Katya: *Et le soir, on peut se retrouver pour manger.*

Sophie: *Bonne idée! Puis on prend le train de 21 heures.*

2. Copy the names of the five places pictured here into your exercise book. Then listen to the tape and write down who is going where and when (morning or afternoon).

A *La tour Eiffel*

B *Un bateau-mouche sur la Seine*

C *La Cité de la Villette*

D *Le Centre Pompidou*

E *Le Marché aux Puces*

3. Listen to Sophie's grandfather explaining how to get to some of the places Sophie and her friends want to visit, starting from the Gare Montparnasse where they will arrive from Nantes.

Match these places with the *métro* stations where they need to get off.

1. *Pour aller au Centre Pompidou, descendez . . .*
2. *Pour aller au Marché aux Puces, descendez . . .*
3. *Pour aller à la Cité de la Villette, descendez . . .*
4. *Pour aller à la tour Eiffel, descendez . . .*
5. *Pour aller à Notre-Dame, descendez . . .*

a) *à la Porte de la Villette.*
b) *à la Porte de Clignancourt.*
c) *à la Cité.*
d) *au Châtelet.*
e) *à Bir-Hakeim.*

Now find all five *métro* stations on the map.

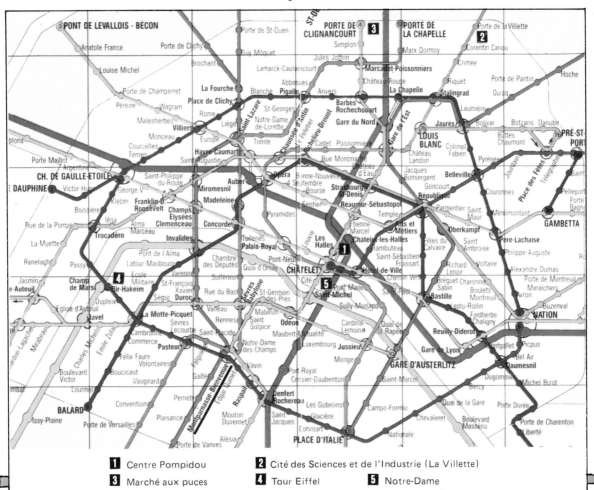

1 Centre Pompidou   **2** Cité des Sciences et de l'Industrie (La Villette)
3 Marché aux puces   **4** Tour Eiffel   **5** Notre-Dame

Cliché RATP

4. Listen to Jean and Sophie making the arrangements for the evening. Work out where they all arrange to meet and at what time.

Avant . . .

5. Listen to Sarah, Katya, Sophie, Jean and Patrick saying what they are going to wear and take with them to Paris. Then find the right set of items for each of them from these pictures.

Après . . .

6. But when they arrived in Nantes, apart from one who had actually found something, they all had either lost something or left something behind. Look carefully at the picture opposite and match each person with the appropriate speech bubble.

Ah, zut! J'ai oublié mon imperméable au restaurant.

Moi, j'ai perdu mon plan de Paris.

Je ne comprends pas. J'ai perdu mon sac..

Ce n'est pas possible. Mon parapluie! J'ai oublié mon parapluie...

Moi, j'ai trouvé un parapluie. C'est ton parapluie ?

Bravo!
OBJECTIFS ATTEINTS

Now you can . . .

. . . explain where something is

C'est à côté de . . .
C'est en face de . . .

. . . say what you would like to do

Je voudrais aller . . .
Je voudrais visiter . . .

. . . arrange where and when to meet

Prends/Prenez l'autobus/le métro . . .
Descends/Descendez . . .
Attends/Attendez . . .

. . . say what you are going to wear or take

Je vais mettre . . .
Je vais prendre . . .

. . . say what you have found, lost or left behind

J'ai trouvé . . .
J'ai perdu . . .
J'ai oublié . . .

Looking at North Africa

LA Reash

SPÉCIALITÉS

COUSCOUS ROYAL 45.50

Couscous is a North African dish made with semolina, a grain a bit like cracked wheat, which is steamed. You can have it with spicy sausages, chicken or lamb and it's served with a vegetable sauce. Katya's family is originally from Alger in Algeria. Many Algerians went to France, because there was more work there and they spoke French as well as Arabic. Most Algerians are Muslims who speak Arabic, but the French invaded Algeria in the 19th century and ruled for over a hundred years. That means that French was used as well as Arabic, although after Algeria gained independence in 1962, many people wanted to go back to using just Arabic.

A number of countries in Africa are French-speaking because the French settled there and ruled them. They're called Francophone countries.

Algeria is a huge country, with a population of only 16½ million. Much of the countryside is desert – very hot and dry most of the year. Morocco and Tunisia are much smaller, but all three countries have become very popular tourist resorts. The climate and the beaches have made them popular . . .

. . . and there are lots of lovely things to buy in the markets or *souks*.

7. Make a list of all the countries that you know of where French is one of the national languages.

8. Can you give reasons why English is spoken in so many different parts of the world?

1. la discothèque

1 Ça commence trop tard	2 Tu as mal au dos	3 C'est trop cher
4 Prends un parapluie	5 Prends le bus. C'est le 6	6 Attends devant la gare

2. le cinéma

1 On va chez ton oncle	2 Tu as trop de devoirs	3 Ton père dit non
4 Prends de l'argent	5 Prends le bus. C'est le 5	6 Attends devant l'hôtel

3. la patinoire

1 Tu n'as pas le temps	2 Ça finit trop tard	3 Tu as mal au ventre
4 Mets une veste	5 Prends le bus. C'est le 1	6 Attends devant le cinéma

4. la plage

1 Tu n'as pas d'argent	2 Tu as mal à la jambe	3 On va chez ta grand-mère
4 Mets un maillot de bain	5 Prends le bus. C'est le 2	6 Attends près du marché

5. le stade

1 Tu dois ranger ta chambre	2 Tu n'as pas envie	3 Tu as mal à la tête
4 Mets un imperméable	5 Prends le bus. C'est le 4	6 Descends en face du château

6. la maison des jeunes

1 Tu es fatigué	2 Tu as trop de devoirs	3 Ta mère dit non
4 Mets un chapeau	5 Prends le bus. C'est le 3	6 Descends en face du musée

Work with a partner. Decide who is partner A and who is partner B.

A. Throw the dice and invite your partner to one of the places numbered 1–6 at the top of each box, according to which number you throw.

B. Throw the dice. If you throw a 1, 2 or 3, you must refuse the invitation, giving the excuse shown in the box of the number you threw. If you throw a 4, 5 or 6 you must accept. (Keep throwing until you get a 4, 5 or 6.)

A. When your partner has accepted an invitation, give him/her the instruction that is indicated in the box of the number that they threw. This will either involve an item of clothing, a bus number or a place to get off the bus.

B. Throw the dice again to try and get the right number of the correct item of clothing that you need (listed in the boxes to the left, the right bus number or the right destination (also listed to the left). If you succeed in throwing the right number at the first try you can claim that you have arrived. Then it is your turn to throw the dice and invite your partner to one of the places, according to the number you throw. (If you do not succeed at the first try, you cannot claim you have arrived.)

The winner is the person who manages to arrive successfully at the most meeting places.

Try these listening activities!

 1. Copy this diagram into your exercise book. Listen carefully to the tape and mark on the diagram all the parts of Michel's body that hurt him.

 2. Fabienne has just flown in from New York and wants to discover what invitations have been left for her on her answering machine. For each invitation, note down in your exercise book:
a) who rings up
b) where they're going
c) when they're going.

 3. Listen to Philippe explaining where to get off the bus to go to some places in town, and write down in your exercise book the names of buildings 1 — 5.

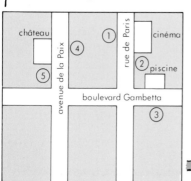

4. Now Philippe is telling people what they are allowed and not allowed to do in town. Unfortunately, he gets some things wrong, as you can see if you compare what he says with this town guide. Follow the numbers on the guide, and note the numbers of the rules that he gets right.

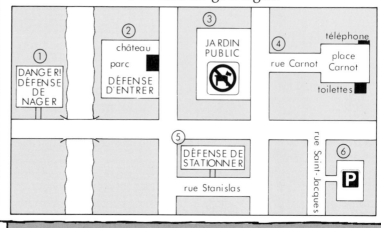

Try these reading activities!

5. Look at this notice board which shows activities organised by the *Maison des Jeunes*. Then decide which one each of the young people will choose, and write down in your exercise book, in figures, the time that he/she will have to meet the others.

6. Which person ought to be particularly interested by each of these advertisements?

Mal à la gorge? Demandez les pastilles Rouge-gorge.

1

VOUS AVEZ CHAUD? MANGEZ UN ESQUIMAU.

2

MAL À LA TÊTE? DEMANDEZ DE L'ASPIRINE.

3

VOUS ÊTES FATIGUÉ? DEMANDEZ LE BAIN-MOUSSANT TONIX.

4

Vous avez froid? Achetez la bouillotte Caout-chaud.

5

A

B

C

D

E

7. Christophe keeps inviting Nadine out, but he keeps getting notes from her saying why she can't come. Put these pictures in the right order from Monday to Friday.

Lundi.
Je suis désolée.
J'ai trop de devoirs.

Mardi.
Je suis désolée.
Je ne peux pas.
Je n'ai pas d'argent.

Mercredi.
Je ne peux pas. On va chez mes grands-parents

Jeudi.
Non. Je n'ai pas le temps.

Vendredi.
Je n'ai pas envie.
OK ?

A

B

C

D

E

Try these writing activities!

8. A pen friend in Paris has invited you to visit him/her. Write back and explain all the things you'd like to do while you're there.

9. Write up a list of rules to be displayed in your classroom. These can be sensible if you like, but they don't have to be.

A

à – at; in; to
il/elle a – he/she has, he's/she's got
il y a – there is; there are
on a – we have, we've got
d'accord – OK
un acteur – actor
une actrice – actress
les actualités – news
    programme
j'adore – I love
adorer – to love
un aéroport – airport
une affaire – thing
l'Afrique – Africa
un âge – age
quel âge as-tu? – how old are you?
ah bon? – really?
j'ai – I have, I've got
j'ai . . . ans – I am . . . years old
aïe! – ouch!
j'aime – I love
aimer – to like
l'Algérie – Algeria
l'Allemagne – Germany
aller – to go
allez! – go on!; come on!
vous allez – you're going
allô – hello
alors – so
américain(e) – American
mon amour – my love
amusant(e) – amusing
amuse-toi bien! -- have a
    good time!
amusez-vous bien! – have a
    good time!
un an – year
l'anglais – English
anglais(e) – English
l'Angleterre – England
un animal – animal
les animaux – animals
un anniversaire – birthday
un anorak – anorak
les Antilles – West Indies
août – August
appeler – to call
il/elle s'appelle – he/she/it is called
je m'appelle – my name is
après-midi – afternoon
une araignée – spider
un arbre – tree
un arbre généalogique – family tree
l'argent – money
une armoire – wardrobe
un arrêt d'autobus – bus stop
arrêter – to stop
tu as – you have, you've got
une aspirine – aspirin
asseyez-vous – sit down
assez – quite
assieds-toi – sit down
une assiette – plate
attendre – to wait

attends/attendez – wait
attends-moi – wait for me
attention! – careful!
au – at; in; to
au revoir – goodbye
au secours! – help!
au troisième top – at the third
    stroke
aujourd'hui – today
aussi – too, also
un autobus – bus
avec – with
une avenue – avenue
vous avez – you have, you've got
avoir – to have
nous avons – we have, we've got
avril – April

B

le babyfoot – table football
le bain – bath
le bain moussant – bubble bath
le ballon – ball
une banane – banana
la banque – bank
le barman – barman
la barre aux céréales – muesli
    bar
la basket – training shoe
le basket – basketball
le bateau-mouche – river boat
    in Paris
bavard(e) – talkative
bavarder – to chat
beau – handsome, beautiful,
    nice
beaucoup – a lot, very much
les beaux-arts – fine arts
belle – beautiful
le bermuda – bermuda shorts
bête – stupid
le beurre – butter
bien – good, well
bien sûr – of course
bienvenue – welcome
la bière – beer
le bifteck – steak
le billet – ticket
la biscotte – French toast
le biscuit – biscuit
bizarre – strange
blanc/blanche – white
bleu(e) – blue
la blouse – overall
le blouson – jacket
bof! – huh! who cares?
boire – to drink
je bois – I drink
la boîte – box
une bombe – spray
bon – good; right
le bonbon – sweet
bonjour – hello
bonne chance – good luck
bonne nuit – good night
bonsoir – good evening

GLOSSARY

la bouche – mouth
la bouillotte – hot water bottle
la boulangerie – baker's shop
le boulevard – wide street
le bouton – spot
le bras – arm
bravo! – congratulations!
le brouillard – fog
le buffet – buffet
le bureau – office
le but – goal

C

ça – this, that
ça fait mal – it hurts
ça va – I'm OK
ça va? – how are you?
le café – café; coffee
le cahier – exercise book
la calculatrice – calculator
le calendrier – calendar
calme – quiet
camper – to camp
le canif – penknife
la capitale – capital city
le cardigan – cardigan
le cartable – satchel, school bag
la carte postale – postcard
la cathédrale – cathedral
ce – this
cela – that
cent – hundred
le centre – centre
le cerf-volant – kite
c'est – this is, it is
c'est-à-dire – that is to say, I
    mean
cet – this
cette – this
la chaine stéréo – stereo system
la chaise – chair
la chambre – bedroom
le champagne – champagne
la chance – luck
changer de place – to change
    seats
le chant – singing
chanter – to sing
le chanteur – singer
la chanteuse – singer
la chanteuse d'opéra – opera
    singer
le chapeau – hat
charmant(e) – charming
le chat – cat
le château – castle
j'ai chaud – I'm hot
chaud(e) – warm, hot
le chauffeur – driver
la chaussette – sock
la chaussure – shoe
la chauve-souris – bat
le chemin – way
la chemise – shirt
la chemise de nuit – nightdress
le chemisier – shirt

cher/chère – dear; expensive
le(s) cheveu(x) – hair
chez – at; to
chez elle – at/to her house
chez lui – at/to his house
chez moi – at/to my house
le chien – dog
la chimie – chemistry
la chip – crisp
le chocolat – chocolate;
    drinking chocolate
choisir – to choose
choisis/choisissez – choose
au chômage – unemployed
le chômage – unemployment
chômeur/chômeuse
    – unemployed
chouette – great
chut! – sshh!
la cigarette – cigarette
le cinéma – cinema
cinq – five
cinquante – fifty
en classe – in the classroom, at
    school
la classe – classroom
classique – classical
le client – client
la cliente – client
le cobaye – guinea pig
le coiffeur – hairdresser
la coiffeuse – hairdresser
la collection – collection
le collège – secondary school
combien? – how much?, how
    many?
comme – like
commencer – to start
comment – how
comment allez-vous? – how
    are you?
comment ça va? – how are
    you?
comment t'appelles-tu?
    – what's your name?
comment vas-tu? – how are
    you?
comment vous appelez-vous?
    – what's your name?
la commode – chest of drawers
comprendre – to understand
je comprends – I understand
la condition – condition
la confiance – confidence
la confiture – jam
content(e) – happy
le copain – friend, pal
copier – to copy
la copine – friend, pal
le corps – body
la Côte d'Ivoire – Ivory Coast
à côté de – next to
la cour – playground
le cours – lesson
le cousin – cousin
la cousine – cousin

la cravate – tie
le crayon – pencil
le croissant – croissant
cruel/cruelle – cruel
en cuir – leather
la cuisine – kitchen; cooking
le cyclisme – cycling

D

dans – in
danser – to dance
le danseur – dancer
la danseuse – dancer
de la – some
décembre – December
déclarer – to declare
défense de – forbidden, not
    allowed
le petit déjeuner – breakfast
le déjeuner – lunch
délicieux/délicieuse
    – delicious
demande/demandez – ask
    (for)
demander – to ask (for)
demi(e) – half
le département – county
dépêche-toi – hurry up
dépêchez-vous – hurry up
derrière – behind, at the back
des – some
descendez – get off; come
    down
descendre – to get off; to
    come down
descends – get off; come
    down
désolé(e) – sorry
le dessert – dessert
le dessin animé – cartoon
dessine/dessinez – draw
dessiner – to draw
à destination de – going to
je déteste – I hate
détester – to hate
deux – two
devant – in front of
devoir – to have to
le devoir – homework
le dimanche – Sunday
le dîner – dinner
dire – to tell, to say
direct – direct
directement – straight
le directeur – director;
    headmaster
la directrice – director;
    headmistress
je dis – I say
dis-moi – tell me
la discothèque – disco
le disque – record
distribuer – to hand out
distribuez – hand out
divorcé(e) – divorced
dix – ten

dix-huit – eighteen
dix-neuf – nineteen
dix-sept – seventeen
le docteur – doctor
je dois – I must
donne/donnez-moi – give me
le dos – back
douze – twelve
du – some

E

une eau – water
une écharpe – scarf
une école – school
une école maternelle – nursery
    school
une école primaire – primary
    school
écoute/écoutez – listen (to)
écouter – to listen to
un écran – screen
écrire – to write
écrivez – write
l'éducation physique
    – physical education
eh bien – well
un(e) élève – pupil
elle – she; it
elles – they
embêter – to annoy
une émission – programme
un emploi – job
mes employés – my staff
en – in
en fait – in fact
encore – still; more
énervant(e) – annoying
un enfant – child
un engin spatial – spaceship
il s'ennuie – he's bored
ennuyeux – boring
entre/entrez – come in
une entrée – starter
entrer – to go in
avoir envie – to feel like
j'ai envie – I feel like
tu es – you are
un esquimau – ice cream
l'Espagne – Spain
est – is
c'est – it is, this is
il est (deux) heures – it's (two)
    o'clock
et – and
vous êtes – you are
étrange – strange
être – to be
euh . . . – er . . .
exactement – exactly
excuse-moi – excuse me
excusez-moi – excuse me

F

en face de – opposite
facile – easy
j'ai faim – I'm hungry

GLOSSARY

faire – to do, to make
faire du vélo – to go for a bike ride
faire la lessive – to do the washing
faire la vaisselle – to do the washing up
faire le lit – to make the bed
faire les courses – to do the shopping
faire les magasins – to go shopping
faire sa valise – to pack a suitcase
faire un tour – to go for a ride/walk
faire une promenade – to go for a ride/walk
je fais mes devoirs – I'm doing my homework
il fait beau – it's beautiful weather
il fait chaud – it's hot
il fait du brouillard – it's foggy
il fait du soleil – it's sunny
il fait du vent – it's windy
il fait froid – it's cold
il fait mauvais – it's bad weather
la famille – family
fantastique – fantastic
fatigué(e) – tired
faux – false
la femme – woman; wife
la femme de ménage – cleaning lady
la fenêtre – window
la fête – festival, Saint's day, holiday
le feu d'artifice – firework
le feuilleton – soap opera, television series
le feutre – felt-tip pen
février – February
la fille – girl; daughter
le film – film
le fils – son
finalement – finally
finir – to finish, to end
le flipper – pinball machine
ils font – they do, they're doing
le football – football
fort(e) – strong; clever
fort(e) en – good at
fou – mad
le français – French
français(e) – French
le frère – brother
le frigo – fridge
la frite – chip
j'ai froid – I'm cold
froid(e) – cold
le fromage – cheese
le fruit – fruit
fumer – to smoke

G

a gagné – has won
gagner – to win
le garage – garage
le garçon – boy
la gare – station
garer – to park
le gâteau – cake
génial – fantastic
la géographie – geography
la girafe – giraffe
la glace – ice cream
la gomme – rubber
la gorge – throat
le gorille – gorilla
la grammaire – grammar
grand(e) – tall, big, large
la grand-mère – grandmother
le grand-père – grandfather
la grande-rue – high street
la Grande-Bretagne – Britain
les grands-parents – grand-parents
la grille – grid
gris(e) – grey
le guide – guidebook
la guitare – guitar

H

j'habite – I live
où habites-tu? – where do you live?
le hamburger – hamburger
une heure – hour, o'clock
le hibou – owl
un hippopotame – hippopotamus
l'histoire – history
une histoire – story
un homme – man
un hôpital – hospital
horrible – awful, horrible
un hôtel – hotel
huit – eight
de bonne humeur – in a good mood

I

ici – here
une idée – idea
il – he; it
ils – they
ils ont – they have
il y a – there is
imbécile – idiot
un imperméable – raincoat
les informations – news
un inspecteur de police – police inspector
intelligent(e) – clever
interdit(e) – forbidden, not allowed
intéressant(e) – interesting
ça m'intéresse – I'm interested
l'Italie – Italy

J

jamais – never
la jambe – leg
le jambon – ham
janvier – January
le Japon – Japan
le jardin – garden
jaune – yellow
je – I
le jean – jeans
le jeu – game, quiz
le jeudi – Thursday
jeune – young
jouer – to play
un jour – day
le/la journaliste – journalist
tous les jours – every day
juillet – July
juin – June
la jupe – skirt
le jus d'orange – orange juice
le jus de fruits – fruit juice

K

le kangourou – kangaroo

L

la – the
là – there; here
le lait – milk
la lampe de poche – torch
le lapin – rabbit
le – the
les – the
la lettre – letter
le lien – bond
la ligne – line
la limonade – lemonade
la liste – list
le lit – bed
le livre – book
loin – far
le lundi – Monday
les lunettes – glasses
le lycée – secondary school
le lycéen – secondary school pupil (boy)
la lycéenne – secondary school pupil (girl)

M

ma – my
la machine à laver – washing machine
madame – madam, Mrs
mademoiselle – Miss
le magasin – shop
le grand magasin – department store
magique – magic
le magnétoscope – video recorder
mai – May
le maillot de bain – swimsuit, trunks
la main – hand
maintenant – now
mais – but
la maison – house
à la maison – at home
la maison des jeunes – youth club
ça fait mal – it hurts
j'ai mal à . . . – my . . . hurts
malade – ill, sick
la maman – mum
la mamie – gran
manger – to eat
le marché – market
le marché aux puces – flea market
le mardi – Tuesday
Mardi gras – Shrove Tuesday
le mari – husband
le mariage – wedding, marriage
marié(e) – married
le Maroc – Morocco
marrant(e) – funny
j'en ai marre – I'm fed up
marron – brown
mars – March
les maths/mathématiques – maths
la matière – subject
le matin – morning
la mémé – gran
la ménagère – housewife
merci – thank you
le mercredi – Wednesday
la mère – mother
mes – my
mesdames – ladies
messieurs – gentlemen
messieurs-dames – ladies and gentlemen
la météo – weather forecast
midi – midday
mignon – cute
minéral(e) – mineral
minuit – midnight
la minute – minute
moche – ugly
moi – I, me
moi non plus – nor me, me neither
moins – less
moins le quart – quarter to
mon – my
monsieur – sir, Mr
le monstre – monster
monter – to go up, to get in
la montre – watch
mort(e) – dead
la moto – motorbike
le mouchoir – handkerchief, tissue
le muguet – lily of the valley
le musée – museum

GLOSSARY

la musique – music
le mystère – mystery

N

nager – to swim
ne . . . pas – not
il neige – it's snowing
neuf – nine
le nez – nose
Noël – Christmas
noir(e) – black
le nom – name
non – no
nous – we; us
nouveau – new
nouvel – new
nouvelle – new
novembre – November
le numéro – number

O

observer – to watch
octobre – October
un œuf – egg
une offre – offer
une oie – goose
un oiseau – bird
on – we
un oncle – uncle
ils/elles ont – they have
onze – eleven
d'or – golden
une orange – orange
un orchestre – orchestra
un ordinateur – computer
une oreille – ear
ou – or
où – where
où habites-tu? – where do
   you live?
où habitez-vous? – where do
   you live?
j'ai oublié – I have forgotten
oublier – to forget
oui – yes
un ours – bear
ouvre/ouvrez – open
un ouvrier – worker
ouvrir – to open

P

pailleté(e) – spangled
le pain – bread
la paire – pair
le pantalon – trousers
la panthère – panther
le papa – dad
Pâques – Easter
le paquet – packet
par – by; through; with
le parapluie – umbrella
parce que – because
le parent – parent
paresseux/paresseuse – lazy
parler – to speak, chat
partir – to leave, to go

pas – not
ne . . . pas – not
on passe – they are showing
passer – to spend
le passe-temps – hobby
la passion – passion
la pastille – lozenge
le pâté – pâté
le patin à roulettes – roller
   skate
la patinoire – skating rink
la pâtisserie – cake
le patron – boss, manager
la pellicule – dandruff
pénible – tedious
perdre – to lose
j'ai perdu – I have lost
le père – father
le père Noël – Father
   Christmas
la permission – permission
perpétuel – everlasting
la personne – person
le petit déjeuner – breakfast
le petit pois – pea
petit(e) – small, little
un peu – a little
je peux – I can; I may
la pharmacie – chemist's
le piano – piano
le pied – foot
le pilote – pilot
le pique-nique – picnic
la plage – beach
le plat – course, dish
il pleut – it's raining
pleuvoir – to rain
le poisson – fish
le poisson rouge – goldfish
le policier – policeman
la pomme – apple
la porte – door
porter – to wear
pose/posez – put down
poser – to put down
la poste – post office
le poste de police – police
   station
le poulet – chicken
la poupée – doll
pour – for; in order to
pourquoi – why
pouvoir – to be able to
nous pouvons – we can
préféré(e) – favourite
préférer – to prefer
premier/première – first
prendre – to take
prends – take
je prends – I take
prenez – take
le prénom – first name
préparer – to prepare
près de – near
principal(e) – main
le prix – price

le problème – problem
le/la prof – teacher
le professeur – teacher
promener – to walk
puis – then
le pull-over – jumper

Q

le quai – quay, embankment
quand – when
quarante – forty
et quart – quarter past
quatorze – fourteen
quatre – four
quatre-vingt-dix – ninety
quatre-vingts – eighty
quel âge as-tu? – how old are you?
quel âge avez-vous? – how old are you?
quel dommage! – what a pity!
quel match! – what a match!
quel/quelle – what, which
quelle heure? – what time?
quelquefois – sometimes
qu'est-ce que . . .? – what . . .?
qu'est-ce que c'est? – what is it?
qu'est-ce que tu as? – what's the matter?
qu'est-ce que tu fais? – what do you do?
qu'est-ce que tu veux? – what do you want?
qu'est-ce que vous voulez? – what do you want?
qui – who
qui est-ce? – who is it?
quinze – fifteen
quitter – to leave
quoi – what

R

la radio – radio
ranger – to tidy; to put away
le rat – rat
la récréation – break
regarde/regardez – look (at)
regarder – to watch, to look at
la règle – ruler
rendez-vous – let's meet
rentrer – to go back
renvoyé(e) – dismissed
le restaurant – restaurant
rester – to stay
retraverser – to cross again
se retrouver – to meet
au revoir – goodbye
rien – nothing
de rien – don't mention it
la rivière – river
la robe – dress
le robot – robot

rouge – red
la rue – street
le rugby – rugby

S

sa – his; her
le sac – bag
tu sais – you know
je ne sais pas – I don't know
la salade – lettuce
la salle à manger – dining room
le salon – sitting room
salut – hi; goodbye
le samedi – Saturday
la sardine – sardine
sauter – to jump
sauvage – unsociable
les sciences – science
scientifique – scientific
au secours – help
secret/secrète – secret
le/la secrétaire – secretary
seize – sixteen
sensationnel/sensationnelle (sensass) – sensational
sept – seven
septembre – September
il sera – it will be
la série – series
le serveur – waiter
la serveuse – waitress
ses – his; her
sévère – strict
si – yes; so
s'il te plaît – please
s'il vous plaît – please
six – six
le slip – briefs
le slip de bain – swimming trunks
le smoking – dinner jacket
la sœur – sister
j'ai soif – I am thirsty
le soir – evening
soixante – sixty
soixante-dix – seventy
le soleil – sun
son – his; her
le sondage – opinion poll
sont – are
ce sont – these are
ils/elles sont – they are
la soupe – soup
sous – under
sportif/sportive – sporty; on sports
le stade – stadium
stationner – to park
la statue – statue
le stylo – pen
sucer – to suck
le sucre – sugar
ça suffit – that's enough
je suis – I am
super – great
le supermarché – supermarket

GLOSSARY

sur – on; about
le survêtement – tracksuit
le sweatshirt – sweatshirt
sympa – friendly, nice
le synthétiseur – synthesiser

T

ta – your
le tabac – tobacconist's shop
la table – table
tais-toi – be quiet
taisez-vous – be quiet
la tante – aunt
tard – late
la tarte – tart
la tartine – slice of bread and
    butter
le tee-shirt – T-shirt
la télé – TV
un téléphone – telephone
téléphoner – to phone
la télévision – television
le temps – time
tes – your
la tête – head
le thé – tea
le théâtre – theatre
tiens – here you are; look
le tigre – tiger
timide – shy
toi – you
les toilettes – toilet
la tomate – tomato
tomber – to fall
ne tombez pas – don't fall
ton – your
ne touche/touchez pas – don't
    touch
toucher – to touch
la tour – tower
tous les jours – every day
tout – everything
tout de suite – immediately
tout le monde – everyone
le train – train
traîner – to hang around
transporter – to carry
le travail – work
travailler – to work
travailleur/travailleuse
    – hard-working
les travaux manuels – craft
traverser – to cross
treize – thirteen
trente – thirty
très – very
trois – three
trop – too
la trousse – pencil case
j'ai trouvé – I have found
trouver – to find
le truc – thing
tu – you

U

un(e) – one; a, an
uni(e) – joined
une usine – factory

V

il/elle va – he/she is going
on va – we're going
je vais – I'm going
la valise – suitcase
varié(e) – varied
les variétés – variety show
tu vas – you're going
vas-y – go ahead
le vase – vase
le vélo – bike
le vendredi – Friday
venez – come
venir – to come
le vent – wind
le ventre – stomach
vert(e) – green
la veste – jacket
je veux – I want
tu veux – you want
je veux bien – I'd love some; I'd
    love to
la viande – meat
le videur – bouncer
la vie – life
viens – come
tu viens? – are you coming?
la ville – town
le vin – wine
vingt – twenty
vite – quickly
voici – here is
voilà – here is, there is; here
    you are
voir – to see
tu vois – you see
la voiture – car
le vol – flight
vos – your
je voudrais – I'd like
on voudrait – we'd like
vous voulez – you want (to)
nous voulons – we want (to)
vous – you
vrai – true
vraiment – really

W

le walkman – personal stereo

Y

y – there
le yaourt – yoghurt
les yeux – eyes

Z

zéro – nil
zut – hell!